ALDFRITH'S BEOWULF

ALDFRITH'S BEOWULF

Translated by
PAULA GRANT

First published in 1995.
Copyright © Paula Grant
Llanerch Publishers.
ISBN 1 897853 98 X.

Also published by Llanerch:

The Saga of King Sverri of Norway,
translated by J. Sephton.

Bandamanna Saga,
translated by John Porter.

Anglo-Saxon Elegiac Verse,
translated by Louis Rodrigues.

Taliesin Poems,
translated by Meirion Pennar.

Northumbrian Crosses of the pre-Norman age,
W. G. Collingwood.

For a complete list of Llanerch Press Ltd publications,
please visit our website: www.llanerchpress.com
or alternatively write to: Llanerch Press Ltd Little Court,
48 Rectory Road, Burnham-on-Sea, Somerset. TA8 2BZ

CONTENTS

INTRODUCTION

This translation of the Beowulf does not differ in its general sense from any other. This is hardly surprising, since the glossaries, dictionary and grammar used have served a great many students of the poem. I have checked it against Garmondsway's (12) translation, with which it broadly agrees, though of course blank verse reads very differently from prose.

The message that I want to convey is, however, different in an important aspect. It is that the Geatish episodes of this Old English masterpiece are not concerned with the Gauts of Sweden, but represent about a hundred years of the history of the Saxon kingdom of Deira – situated in what is now Yorkshire and Durham. Having said that, it does seem likely that they shared some of their ancestors with the Swedish Gauts, but in a period earlier than the one studied here.

Our period falls mainly between the 450s and the 550s AD though there are references to earlier events and people: the Eormenric of line 1200, for instance, died in 376 AD while the exile and slavery foretold at lines 3017/18 and elsewhere belong to the second half of the sixth century and the beginning of the seventh.

The two parts of Northumberland were separated before our period into Deira and Bernicia (2), but even after they were reunited under King Ida, the name Northumbria/Northumberland does not seem to have been used. Adamnan in his Life of Columba (quoted by John Marsden p.205) (23) calls the territory Saxonia, the Danish medieval historian Saxo Grammaticus calls it Saxland, and the Book of Leinster calls it Saxonaib (also quoted by John Marsden p.66).

The first Geatish ruler to arrive in Deira was the distinguished Roman general Hosidius Geta (25), who came with the 9th (Hispanic) Legion in 43 AD. The Geatish homeland was then the lower Danube which flows into the Black Sea. The emperor

2

Claudius ordered his most senior general, Aulus Plautius, to set up the invasion of Britain, which Claudius would join later. Plautius was in Pannonia (roughly modern Austria) when he received the order. The nearest legion was the 9th, so Plautius sent for it and made his way to the channel ports, collecting three other legions on the way.

When the invasion of Britain had been accomplished, the legions spread out: the 9th went to the Humber region, it was based upon Lincoln and later upon York and is thought to have remained in Britain for the rest of the century. 'Foundations of "citizen colonies" developed as legionaries retired' (Salway) (17). This is not to suggest that the entire legion was composed of Geats, they were after all 'Hispanic' but yet there may have been some Geatish followers of Hosidius among the retiring veterans.

Two hundred years later any Geatish families in the region must have got a boost to their prestige when the Roman Emperor Serverus left his second son, Geta, to administer the government of Britain while he fought in Scotland.

None of this alters the likelihood that the Beowulf's Geats were descended from the ancestors of the Gauts of Sweden, as is indicated by the Anglo-Saxon Chronicle's pedigree of King Ida of Northumbria; however, the name Geat had long been associated with power and prestige in Deira.

Deira lay between the rivers Humber and Tyne. It flourished from about half way through the fifth century, but during the sixth it lost its separate identity and fell beneath the rule of its neighbours – first of East Anglia for a few years, then as part of a reunited Northumbria under King Ida (547-559).

The Geats fit these circumstances sufficiently well for us to look for further connections. One rather important link appears in the name Swerting for Hygelac's ancestor (line 1203). In a passage about the kings of Deira, the British writer Nennius (2) starts at the beginning: 'Woden genuit Beldeyg. Brond genuit

3

Siggar, genuit Sebald, genuit Zegulf, genuit Soemil. Ipse primus separavit Deur o Birneich. Soemil genuit Sguerthing...' And so on. Siggar is probably the same as Siggeir of Gautland who is found in some pedigrees, that takes care of the Gaut ancestors. Now look at Soemil, he 'first separated Deira from Bernicia' and his son is called Sguerthing/Swerting (GU in British meant the same as W). It cannot be gainsaid that there was a connection between Deira and Swerting, the ancestor of the Beowulf's Geatish kings. The Danish historian Saxo Grammaticus calls Swerting king of Saxland. That fits well, Northumbria was sometimes known as Saxonia (Adamnan's Life of Colomba), and 'Saxonaib' (Book of Leinster) (23).

Another link is that the Geats are often referred to in the poem as 'Weder Geats' or just plain 'Weder' and 'Wederer' (line 1894 for example). The second centry Greek geographer Ptolemy of Alexandria had produced a map of Britain in which he named the river Wear the 'Vedra' (5). Virtually the same word. The Wear lies on Deira's northern side close to the river Tyne which formed the boundary. Copies of Ptolemy's map would have been of special interest to pilgrims to Rome from Britain, but in any case, it would probably have been copied and brought here in Roman times for use by the generals.

A very important Geatish character in the Beowulf is Eafer, or Eofor (The Boar). This young man slew Ongentheow, married the daughter of the Geatish King Hygelac, and was given a great deal of land and riches. It seems quite likely that Eofor took his name from the city of York, which the Saxons called Eaferwiccaester (Boar-wick-castle) (15). In Roman times York had been called Eburacum and was the second city in the land after London; the name meant 'Yew Tree' but the Saxons probably decided it was their word meaning 'Boar'. The Geats would have regarded a name with Boar as one of its elements as highly auspicious because they were of Gothic descent and boars were significant in their culture.

4

One more thing worth noticing is the use of the word 'brentings' at line 2806. This is usually translated 'sailors', but I have left it untranslated because as it is, it is probably cognate with 'Brigantes' (26) or 'Brigantians' the people who lived in Northumbria in Roman times (when it included Deira) and who still lived there although now they were ruled by Geatish Kings. In the poem Y Gododdin (13) the poet Aneirin remarks that the English army was a mixed force (899).

A help in understanding that the Geats were Deirans is the text of the Beowulf itself. There are three passages which foretell exile or slavery as the impending fate of the Geats. Lines 2884-2887 prophesy that they will lose their hold on their land: 'Now shall endowments and sword gifts, all joys of home, love of your kindred, cease. Must each man's land-right of this tribe become void, when Kings afar do learn your shame...' At lines 3017-3018 exile is foreseen: '...in sorrowful mood, bereft of gold, often, not once, shall tread strange land'. And at lines 3150-3154 an old woman - a priest perhaps - laments: '...much her remaining days bewailed, that dreaded she, with murder filled, men defeated, humbled and enslaved.'

Deira, more than most countries, had a tradition of exile and slavery during the sixth and early seventh centuries. The most famous tale is that of Pope Gregory the Great (died 604 AD). The Pope sees some fair-haired captives taken as slaves; he inquires 'what men are these?' When told they are Angles, he makes the well-known remark 'not Angles, but Angels'. A version of the story goes on: 'where are they from?' asks the Pope. 'From Deira, my lord.' 'Then', says the pun-loving pontiff, 'we must save them from Dei ira' (the wrath of God, because they were pagans). Sir Frank Stenton (18) in his Anglo-Saxon England leaves out the second part of the story, but he does connect the tale with Deira.

In addition, churchmen liked to point to the exile of King Edwin of Deira which by coincidence ended when he accepted Christianity. Such was the climate in which our poet wrote.

(Marsdon).

There would be no difficulty in accepting a Geatish Deira were it not for the Swedish kings Ongentheow and his son Ohter. Taking Ongentheow first, an important observation is made by Sr G. Turville-Petre: 'The old King of the Swedes, Ongentheow... has not been identified in the Norse sources. It might be expected that his name in Norse would be something like Angantyr, but no such name occurs in the list of kings of the Swedes' (27).

There was, however an Angantyr son of Heithrek in Hervor and Heithrek's Saga (8). The story is medieval, but is said to show signs of being much older, at least in part. Heithrek killed his brother and so was exiled to the northern forests for seven years. After that he was permitted to take a ship and seek his fortune abroad with a handful of followers. He went to the court of the Scylding king and fought his battles so successfully that the king gave him his daughter Helga in marriage and half the kingdom to rule. Their son was Angantyr, who could be the Ongentheow of the Beowulf; he may never have seen Sweden in his life. The land was stricken by famine and it was decided to sacrifice Angantyr to the Gods to appease them. Heithrek prevented this by slaying the king and Halfdane, his son. Helga killed herself and Heithrek took over the whole kingdom of the Danes.

Heithrek led the Danes into what is now Denmark and met a force under Withergield – this is most likely the Jute Whitgils, the father of Hengest (6). There was a battle, Withergield was slain, the surviving Jutes were taken prisoner. It appears from the Beowulf that Ecgtheow, grandson of Withergield, was among the prisoners (lines 460-472). The Beowulf poet now seems to draw upon the Saga of Heithrek Wolfskin (28) (lines 460-472 in Beowulf) where the prisoners rise up and slay Heithrek; the poet has it that they are led by Ecgtheow. Now at the height of his power, Heithrek is killed. He was ruler over Norway, Denmark and possibly tribes such as the Ingevones whose lands were close by. At his father's death, Angantyr might call himself king over all these territories, but in practice he could not hold any of them.

Ecgtheow had reinstated the Scylding dynasty and called his own son Beowulf after the first non-mythological Scylding king, to commemorate his, Ecgtheow's, own exploit. Angantyr must flee. Where could he go? The Danes were now mortal enemies. In Norway he was wanted as a sacrifice to the Gods, in Sweden Froda was king. From the Saga of Frithiof (10) (also fairly late, I believe) it seems that Angantyr went to the Orkneys where the Scylding king Helgi sent a demand for tribute. Angantyr paid it, but very soon (switching now to Nennius) (2) he must have been driven out by 'a son and a nephew of Hengest' who came to devastate the islands. If Ongentheow was Angantyr the son of Heithrek, then plainly he had no choice but to throw in his lot with the Picts or Britons. And so we find him in Britain, claiming to be the King of Sweden.

The Picts and the Britons had a custom that kings and princes often took their titles through the female line. If Ongentheow could have a son by a queen or princess of those peoples, he, as her consort would command the loyalty of her warriors, and his son would be at least a prince, finally with luck a king. And so, by a lady called Bryd, Ongentheow has a son called Ohter by the English, "Ottar" and "Otr" by the Norse, and Arthur (14) by the Britons in later medieval legends.

More can be discovered about the Geats by studying Hygelac's Queen. The poet calls her Hygd and adds that she was 'Haereth's daughter' (line 1929). He also says that her son was 'nefa Hereric's' (line 2207). Hereric is likely to have been on Hygd's side of the family, because Hygelac's antecedents are known. The poet likes all his characters who were related or allied to have alliterative names – H in this case – so Hereric could just as likely have been Ereric, and Haereth, Aereth or Erth. In Chronicle of the Picts and Scots MCCLI (MS Brit.Mus.Harl.4628) published by W.F. Skene in his Pictish Chronicles (3), a number of versions is given of the name of Erc, a fifth century king of the Dalriadic Picts of Northern Ireland: the list includes Erc, Eric, Erth, Her, Herc, Herth. The last name, pronounced with Scottish definition of consonants, is Haereth. This makes it likely that the poet's Hereric is Erc. He has made King Erc and King Haereth father and son, whereas the Chronicle makes them one person, but the family was large, Erc had several sons whose names all ended in 'Mac Erc', so any error is not great.

British, Pictish and Scottish princes often took their titles from their mothers. Many sources mention this, including Bede, but another source is a verse from the Pictish additions to Nennius's Historia Britonum (2):

There were oaths imposed on them,
By the stars, by the earth,
That from the nobility of the mother
Should always be the right to the sovreignty.
(Verse 30)

This meant that an Anglic king such as Hygelac of Geats could, by marrying such a princess, obtain the allegiance of her subjects and that his son would be regarded by the Picts as a Pictish prince or perhaps king, no matter from what people his father came. Queens, therefore, were of great political importance; an Angle, Geat or a Swede married to a Pictish or British queen would have the allegiance of her subjects without having to fight for it. In the case of Hygd, we have seen that she was a Scot - daughter of the High King of Northern Ireland. Any followers of Queen Hygd therefore would owe allegiance to Hygelac. This situation seems to be confirmed by the Danish writer Saxo Grammaticus who, speaking of Hugleik's (Hygelac's) last battle, makes him leader of the Irish. Foreigners could not always distinguish Scots from Irish.

A word more about Hygd: at line 1943 she is said to be peerless. At line 1951 her father, Haereth, has no difficulty in arranging a second marriage for her with a powerful young king despite the plight of the Geatish realm. It appears that she had become the paramount Queen in Britain, a lady without peer – she had no social equal. In this context it is important to remember that she had a daughter who had been given in

8

marriage (probably as a child) to Eafor, the slayer of Ongentheow (line 2998). One day, therfore, Eafor would be the husband of an extremely royal princess, perhaps to be paramount in her turn. He would be a king.

The Beowulf's Eafer/Eofor ('the Boar') is, more likely than not, King Ida of Northumbria (6). Ida's dates are usually taken in Bede and the Anglo-Saxon Chronicle to have been 547-559. So he only became king for the last twelve years of his life. He had a great many sons – six of them by his wife – so it seems likely that he lived a long time. It would be reasonable to suppose that he was born in, or soon after 480. His dates therefore fit the young Eafer who slew Ongentheow in 500 or 505. It would not be at all surprising if, on the death of Queen Hygd, Eafer's wife became the object of British, Scottish or Pictish allegiance. Ida/Eafer would have become king of all the territories between the Forth and the Humber. Indeed his very name – Ida – seems to suggest that: 'ides' meant 'lady, woman' in Anglo-Saxon. In the Anglo-Saxon Chronicle's 853 AD (Parker A) (6) pedigree of Aethelwulf, Ida's name is Eafa. Meanwhile under Anglo-Saxon rule, York had become Eaferwiccaester (15).

At the beginning of his career, then, Eafer slays Ongentheow; by the end of it, he is King of the whole of Northumbria. What happened in between? Here it is as well to note that Eafer's name alliterates with Eanmund and Eadgils and to remember that our poet likes to use alliteration to indicate allies as well as kinsmen; no doubt he was involved in the wars that led to the deaths of Eanmund and Heardred and the departure from these shores of Eadgils. So much for the English sources. What about the British? Did they keep no memory of their old enemy? It would be strange if the death of Ongentheow were to pass unavenged – not only was he a claiment to the throne of Sweden, he was also the great war-leader the Britons called Uther.

The name 'Uther' appears to have been a nick-name, the Welsh dictionary of Evans and Thomas (29) gives 'uthr' as meaning 'awful'. The Beowulf at line 2929 calls Ongentheow 'egesful' meaning 'terrible'. The saga of Hervor and Heithrek (8) mentions that some of Heithrek's forebears and he himself were subject to berserk rages. If Ongentheow is Heithrek's son Angantyr, then it seems possible that he may have inherited the same peculiarity and so acquired the adjective uthr as a nick-name.

The Britons knew of a Boar; he appears as the enemy of Arthur and as a war leader of considerable resourcefulness when it came to getting out of a tight spot. He is the Twrch Trwyth son of Taredd who fights a long series of battles against Arthur in the Mabinogion's (14) tale of Culhwch and Olwen. 'Twrch' means 'boar' the rest of the name is a coarse insult. The story is told of how Arthur's allies went north against a boar called 'Ysgithyrwyn Chief Boar' that meant, probably, that he wore a tusk or tusks on his helmet. They kill him, in fact they split his head in two. Then they retire to Cornwall, seemingly to gather information about where the second enemy leader, Twrch, had gone; they find he has gone to Ireland, they follow, there is a battle against the Irish which Arthur wins, he returns to Dyfed in Wales and gathers together a much larger army. With this he invades Ireland again, locates the Boar and fights with him but the result is inconclusive and he attempts to treat with the Boar. The Boar promptly boards his ship and returns to Wales with Arthur close behind him. They land at Dyfed, the Boar retreats to Preseleu. There is a battle near Glyn Nyfer which the Boar wins, but is himself wounded.

There is a series of skirmishes, all of which seem to be won by the Boar and his ally Grugyn. The Boar and Grugyn separate, Grugyn goes to Cardigan but here his luck runs out and he is slain. But the Boar soldiers on, eventually he is located and driven toward the river Severn; at the river he barely escapes with his life, but somehow manages to flee to Cornwall, Arthur follows but the Boar escapes by sea and the tale ends.

In the story of Culhwch and Olwen (14) the Boar is said to wear upon his head a comb (22), scissors and a razor. This gives us some idea of what the war was about: earlier in the story Culhwch goes to Arthur to declare loyalty and ask Arthur's help.

10

As a token of his becoming Arthur's man, he asks Arthur to cut his hair. This meant that, although related to Arthur, he did not consider himself in line for the throne. This custom lasted a long time: for instance in France a Queen Clothild (30), mother of the Kings Childebert and Lothar, kept her grandsons' hair long because cutting it would have indicated that they had no claim to the throne.

It seems likely that by flaunting these ceremonial hair-cutting implements, the Boar was inviting leaders of the Britons to swear allegiance to himself and not to Arthur; at the same time he is saying to Arthur 'stop me if you can'. If he didn't flaunt the comb etc (22), Arthur was prepared to ignore him, the tale makes that clear. It seems then that the war was to see who could collect the allegiance of the petty kings sufficiently to unite the whole island of Britain.

The authorship of the Beowulf cannot be proven, but John Marsden in his Northanhymbre Saga (23), reports a proposal by an American Professor Albert S. Cook that it was commissioned by King Aldfrith of Northumbria, 685-705 AD, the eldest son of King Oswy. John Marsden was able to bring Cook's work together with the later collateral researches of Professor Carney, and with his own studies and his interest in Aldfrith's tutor, Adamnan, was able to suggest King Aldfrith himself as the author of the poem. A very great discovery indeed and one which I respectfully accept.

I have mentioned the Beowulf's references to exile in its closing passages. Aldfrith lived until he was over forty as an exile because, although he was his father's eldest son, he had been declared to be illegitimate and was passed over in favour of his half-brother. He was a poet in both English and Irish, Marsden says 'his Irish poetry still extant demonstrates a remarkable competence in the rigorous disciplines of the Celtic bards.' He was also familiar with the Iliad judging by his description of Beowulf's funeral. Aldfrith, then, had the time and the talent to have written the Beowulf, he would also have had the historical

11

knowledge, since all the characters in the Geatish episodes were his ancestors or their kin. His mother was Irish, and, Marsden says, he spent some years on the island of Iona (23).

Below is a pedigree for Aldfrith based on the Eafer-Ida identification. Eafer's wife is not named in the poem, it just says she was given in marriage to Eafer (line 2997). John Marsden gives the name of Ida's wife as Bearnoch (23), this from 'genealogies interpolated into the Nennian Northern History...'

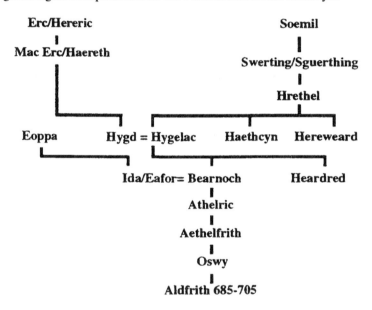

Professor Cook and John Marsden regard Aldfrith as author of the poem Widsith (12). I would propose that he was also the author of Deor, a short poem bewailing exile, where the poet says 'Deor is my name' (12). The Latin for Deira was Deur (2). In calling himself Deira-Deur-Deor, he seems to use the Gaelic mode, 'The Deira' as one might say 'The Maclaren' or 'The O'Neil'. Aldfrith became king at last when he was forty-one; he was at last 'Deor'.

The poem follows in crude translation. Those passages which have explanatory notes are marked *.

12

ALDFRITH'S BEOWULF

1   What we from Gardanes in yore days learned
     Of the might of nations' kings,
     How chieftains then performed great deeds.

*   Often Scyld Scefing with martial host
5   Seized the throne of many a tribe,
     Subdued the earl.
     By poverty was driven from the first,
     Thus did he to prosper bide,
     Waxed in the world.
     Thrived so in honour that peoples neighbouring
10   Across the sea should hear – tribute rendering –
     Great was that king.
     Later a son was born to him,
     An heir in the court God sent to men's aid,
15   Hard times they had lived through, leaderless long.
     Him the all-glorious, life-giving Lord
*   Granted world-honour, Beowulf was famed;
     Far sprang his glory, Scyld's son in Scane.

20   A young man of rank shall so behave -
     Free with rewards in his father's home,
     That men beside him stand in age,
     Comrades willing, when battle comes,
     To serve the land. Great deeds shall in nations
25   Everywhere prosper a man.

*   When Scyld's fated hour drew near
     Awesome the voyage in Frean was:
     They took him to the ocean shore
     As he bade his comrades close
30   While Scyld had yet the power of words,
     Long-loved chieftain of the land.

     There, stem-swept, in harbour stood,
     Icy and out-bound, the atheling's craft;

| | They laid their dear leader, giver of treasure, |
| 35 | In the ship's bosom, close by the mast. |

With riches from far, with ornaments dressed,
I heard of no ship more comely adorned,
40 War-sword and corselet laid on his breast,
Goods without number to be with him borne
In flood's far possession away.

No less the offering on him they bestowed
45 Than had they who first sent him forth as a child
Alone on the tide; moreover they set
A banner of gold high over his head,
Let the wave carry off their gift to the deep.

Sad their hearts, their spirits grieved,
50 Not wise men nor heroes truly can say
Who under heaven that cargo received.

In the strongholds Beowulf was then
Scyldings' dear king, folk-famous long,
55 His father departed, the leader from home.
Thence he awoke high Halfdane in turn,
As long as he lived, war-fierce and old,
The Scylding lord.
*   From four descendants forth recounted
60 Warrior chieftains in the world awoke:
Heorogar and Hrothgar and Halga the good
Heard I that the noble queen
Graced the bed of Heatho Scilfing.

Hrothgar then was given war-speed, high esteem,
That readily his comrades followed him
65 Till many henchmen swelled his youthful band.
Came mood that he a palace would command,
A greater dwelling built by men
70 Than ever heard the wisest one, and therein
Deal out to old and young

All that God had given him,
Except the common land and lives of men.

Then wide the work ordained, I heard,
75   Many a tribe throughout this earth
The folk-stead ornamenting; soon they came
Prompt with men, that, completed, it became
The greatest hall – Heorot by the poet named
Whose words wide powers held.
80   His vow not unfulfilled – treasures, jewels, shared,
Rose up the hall, high and horn-gabled.
*   (Wars fires awaited, flames of wrath;
Not long was it that bitter hatred, violent death
85   An uncle with his nephew yet to war should wake.)

*   An envious demon angry raged,
Counting days he revels heard
Loud in the hall: there was music of harps,
90   Clear sang the poets, telling the tale
Of earliest times, of the coming of men:
How by the Almighty the earth was created
Fair to behold, with ocean surrounded,
Of sun's and moon's victorious birth,
95   Lanterns to lighten the dwellers on earth;
And, as is taught, to the land he gives
Branch and leaf, all that lives,
All things fitting, all that moves.

So the warriors lived merrily on,
100 Happy, although a certain one
Waited to wrong – a hellish fiend
Was that grim spirit, Grendel named,
That haunted the marshes, held the moors,
Fen and fastness, the lands of trolls.
105 A while did the wretch remain
When him his Maker had condemned
In kind as Cain.
(That crime the Lord avenged again

Thus, that he had Abel slain
No prize of war, but banishment far
110   Ordained for his guilt from the race of men.
Thence woke all seeds of wickedness:
Eoten and Ylfing and Orcneas,
Long years such monsters warred with God –
He paid their debt.)

115   With coming of night he neared the hall –
How had the Ring-Danes defended it
After drinking their ale? Then found within
The courtier bands asleep after feasting,
Sorrow unknowing – the wretched men!
120   The ghoul unhallowed, avid and grim
Was the readier then. Savage and cruel
He fell upon thirty thanes at rest within.
With loot triumphant homewards went,
125   Back to his lair, death-satisfied.

When in the half-light of dawn
Was shown Grendel's war-craft to men,
Then after feasting the sound of great weeping
Was lifted up loud in the morning.
130   Sad sat the noblest of kings,
Grieved for his sorrowing thanes

When they saw the dread tracks of a Being accursed.
The struggle too strong,
Fearful and long; no more did he wait
But scarcely one night, with murder again
135   And merciless, feared and ferocious
Was fast upon them.

Then easily found was he who elsewhere
More roomily resting, slept in the byre.
140   When he was beaconed the signal bright
Told truly a hall-thane's punishment
Held toward him when safe and afar

The foe he escaped.

So he triumphed and strove with right,
145   One against all, while idle stood the royal house.
Long was it so, twelve troubled winter-tides
Lord Scyld endured, each full of woe
Bitterness and grief, for everyone,
150   Both old and young, most clearly knew
The dismal tale: that Grendel warred
With Hrothgar long, for years the bloody war
155   Dragged on, nor would make peace with any of the Danes,
Nor pay blood-money to remove the stains,
No bright redress came from the slayer's hands
But endless persecution, for the ghoul
160   Hung like a death-shade over old and young;
Endless night lurked on the misty moors
(Where rove Hell's wizards, no man knows).

165   So men's cruel foe the grim lone-ganger
Often repeated his dreadful crimes,
Heorot the treasure hall knew blackest night.
He must not – rich before the Judge –
Approach the Throne, nor divine His Intent!
That was Scyld's great punishment,
Pride's bringing down.

Many a chief in council sat,
Pondered advice – what deed was best
To do against surprise attack?
175   Whiles at the temple they
For aid to the gods appealed,
To idols against disaster
Chanted aloud. (Their way was such –
Of heathen hopes, hellish belief,
180   In spirit knowing not God, our Judge,
Nor Truth, nor Heaven's love,
Nor praising the Creator of the world.
Woe to him that shall

17

Through practice dire thrust his soul
185 In fire's abyss.
Solace let him not expect, wandering wight.
Well to him that may
Seek the Lord beyond death's day
And to the Father plead
For peace.)

So the unhappy times dragged on
For Halfdane's heir, continuing war,
190 Nor could the wisest avert disaster,
The struggle too strong, cruel and long,
On the people came bloodshed, murder
And terror-by-night.

From his home a thane of Hygelac
Learned of Grendel's deeds.
195 Powerful among the Geats,
Strongest all the days he lived,
Princely and great. He had a ship
Well fitted out, quoth he would seek
The famous prince, the warrier king
200 Across the sea, and needed men.

Small blame to him from prudent friends
Though him they loved;
Encouraged, Valour looked for Luck.
205 This leader had from Geatish land
Picked the keenest he could find –
Some fifteen men the vessel sought,
The sea-skilled swordsman knew the coast.
210 First forth they went. Afloat on waves
The boat lay under cliffs. Eager braves
Stepped on the prow, currents churned
With sand the Sound. On the ship's beam brightly shone
215 The gear of war by warriors borne.
Men shoved off the loaded bark,
Friends in willing enterprise.

18

Went they over billows, wind-borne,
Floated foamy-prowed as sea-birds,
220   Till another day in time
The vessel's curving stem had sailed
That sighted they the gentle land:
Bright cliff shining, steep hill towering,
Spacious capes, then sea was sailed,
Their journey's end. Thence upward swift
225   (The ship made fast) ascended to the plain
With armour jingling, mailed shirts;
Thanks to God the Wederers gave
That smoothed their passage over wave.

When from the wall the Scylding guard saw
230   (He who the coast-watch should hold)
Borne down the gangway shining bright shields
All ready for battle, his interest roused,
Wondering what men were those?
235   Then riding his horse, Hrothgar's thane want,
Stoutly grasping his spear, to enquire:

'What are ye warriors, mail-clad soldiers
That this tall ship brings here over seas?
240   Not while the coast-guard watch I held
That none might come with pirate band
To raid upon the Danish land
Came warriors venturing here more blatantly!
245   Not ye the soldiers' pass-word,
The tribe's permission utterly unknown!
(I never saw a grander earl on earth
Than is someone of your troop in arms -
That is no serf bedecked with weapons
250   Unless him his matchless looks belie.)
Now I shall know
What people you are from before you go
Further to spy upon the Danish land.
255   Now you foreigners – sea-rovers –

19

My advice is plain: haste is best
To make known whence you came.'

The eldest answered him, the leader
Unlocked words' treasury:

260   'We are men of the Geats and Hygelac's household,
My father was famed among folk,
A noble prince called Ecgtheow
Who lived many winters ere he passed
265   Aged from court. In the wide world
Every wise man well remembers him.
We come in friendship, thy great Lord,
Halfdane's son, to seek; be thou our guide
270   We have an errand to the Danish prince.
Nor shall it be secret: I daresay
Thou knowest if it is true, as we have heard,
That someone wars with Scyldings,
275   A mystery killer at dead of night

'Horribly attacks – uncanny, brutish,
Hideous and bloodthirsty. I this Hrothgar may
Through generous-hearted council teach
How he – firm and great – the foe defeats
280   If he the baleful onslaught ever should repulse
Relief comes soon, and care's fire burns cooler then.
Or else disaster ever more,
Hard times as long yet will endure
285   As upright stands the royal house.'

The guard spoke where on horse he sat,
Insolent official:
'Shrewd warriors, who well perceive
Shall a-judge twixt word and deed.
290   This I hear, that this war-band
is faithful to the Scylding Lord.
Go forward, bearing arms and mail,
I guide you. Further I command

295　My thanes to moor upon the sand
　　　Your fresh-caulked ship against all harm
　　　Held safely, till the wooden arc
　　　Next conveys a vaunted man
　　　Across the sea to Wedermark
　　　(Granted be such a daring-doer
300　Emerges whole from the rush of war).

　　　He turned to go. The ship lay still,
　　　Her cable rode, steep-sided, broad,
　　　At anchor fast; boar's likeness shone
　　　Above the face-bearing, inlaid with gold,
305 *　Adorned and fire-hard, the life-watch held.

　　　Men in haste together marched
　　　Till they could see the splendid hall –
　　　That was foremost under heaven –
310　Wherein the ruler dwelt, a light
　　　Shining over many lands.

　　　The soldier pointed out to them
　　　The chieftain's house, that they to him
　　　Might entrance gain.
315　Some warrior turned his horse and quoth:
　　　'Time is for me to go.
　　　Father of the world, with grace
　　　Keep your adventure sound!
　　　I will to the sea – hold guard
　　　Against invading bands.'

320　Stone-paved the street was,
　　　They trooped along the way,
　　　Hand-locked, hard, the armour shone,
　　　The clink of mail a battle song.
　　　Then those foremost at the hall
　　　In their grim war-gear sat
325　Sea-weary beside their shields,
　　　The tempered discs against the wall.

On benches set, the birnies clanked,
Soldiers' armour, spears together stood,
Seamen's arms, ash-wood from grey above,
330   Weapon-rich was this iron host.
Then a haughty warrior
Enquired from the leader:
'Wherefor, spearmen, bear ye shields stout,
Grey shirts of mail and visored helms?
335   I am Hrothgar's spokesman and his herald.
I never saw so many valiant foreigners;
I presume that ye in courtesy, not exile,
But in goodwill have sought Hrothgar?'

340   Then loftily him answered the proud Wederer Lord,
Spoke next in words stern under helm:
We are of Hygelac's household, Beowulf is my name.
345   My errand I will tell to Halfdane's son,
The famous prince thy Lord, if he will grant
That we as noblemen may greet him.'

Wulfgar spoke, that was chief of Wendals,
His nature was known to everyone -
350   Warlike and wise: 'I will ask the Friend of Danes,
The Scylding Prince, Giver of Wealth
As thou desirous art, great chief,
Touching thy venture, and to thee then
Make at once the answer known
355   That me the leader thinks to give.'

Then quickly went where Hrothgar sat
Old and grey amidst his earls,
Gracefully moved, that he before
The Danish prince's shoulder stood
(He knew the customs of the court)
360   Wulfgar addressed his overlord:

'Here are come people from the Geats,
Travelled far across the sea;

The eldest is called Beowulf,
They ask that they, my lord, with thee
365 May words exchange.
Deny not answer to this company
Good Hrothgar, they are armed as earls;
The leader is valiant moreover
370 Who brings this war-troop hither.'
Hrothgar spoke, the Lord of Scyldings:
'I knew him when he was a boy!
His father was named Ecgtheow
The one whom Hrethel Geats
375 Gave his only daughter. Is his offspring now
Hard come hither? Desired friendship?
Those sailors said, who brought good-will gifts
From the Geats, that he'd the might of thirty men
380 In the grip of his one hand.
Holy God sends us him for help
To West Danes against Grendel's war!
I have expected this.
385 For his daring I shall reward the champion.
Be thou in haste, call entrance,
See the friendly troop together,
Say them words withal – that they are welcome
To the realm of Danes.'

390 The entry word proclaimed:
'My Lord of East Danes orders told to you
That he your family knows,
And ye by him are welcome here
From over sea with hard resolve.
391 Now ye may go in helm and mail
To see Hrothgar, let shields here
Abide the meeting, also spears.'

Then arose the leader
400 With his gallant band of thanes,
Some stayed behind to guard the arms
As the captain did command,

The rest in haste followed their guide
Beneath Heorot's roof. Stern under helm
401 Where he stood upon the hearth, Beowulf spoke,
His mail shone, the war-net sewn
With craftsman's art.

'Be thou, Hrothgar, hail!
I am Hygelac's kin and thane.
In youth I have many a venture braved:
To me the Grendel thing became
410 In my homeland clearly known;
Sailors say that this great hall
Stands bereft of comrades, all
Idle and undefended when
Evening light hides under cloak of heaven.
415 Urged me then my people –
Most prudent councillors –
Prince Hrothgar, that I seek thee,
For they know my skill in war.
Saw themselves when I from battle came
420 Bloodstained in the fray where Fife I bound,
Wiped out the giants' race and slew at sea
Night's devils of the deep in narrow escapade,
Avenged the wrongs of Wederers,
Looked for danger, crushed the foe,
And with Grendel shall I now
425 Alone against that fiend prevail,
Settle with the cannibal.
Now I will beg thee, Prince of Danes,
Noble Lord Scylding, one boon
That thou reject me not, leader of men,
430 Ruler of nations, now I thus far have come,
That I may alone of my earl troop,
This gallant group, Heorot cleanse.

'Also have I learned that this arch-demon
In his frenzy careth not for arms.
435 I that then scorn! As for me,

24

Hygelac, being my lord, is pleased
That I bear sword or shield broad,
The yellow roundel to the fight,
'But my bare hands shall grip the foe
And in close mortal combat meet
440   Hate with hatred, where shall trust
The one death takes – that God is just.

'I know that he will, if his strength allows,
Consume the Geats in the battle hall
Without remorse, as he often did
445   The flower of men before. No need for thee
To hide my head, but me he will have dearly bloodied
If me death claims – the gory corpse he bears away
450   Thinking to devour; the lone-ganger's remorseless meals
Mark the lair in the moor.
Nor needst thou sorrow long
About my body's place of rest,
Send to Hygelac on if war takes me
The mail that I wear upon my breast,
*   Fine corselet that Hrethel left – Weland's work.
455   Goes Fate ever as it must.'

Hrothgar spoke, the Lord of Scyldings:
'In defence, my comrade Beowulf,
And in kindness thou has sought us.
*   Thy father struck most fiercely,
460   His hand brought death to Heatholaf
Midst Wilfings, then the warrior's kin
For battle terror could not hold him.
Thence he sought the South Dane folk
Over rolling waves, the Scylding chief,
465   When first I ruled the Danish folk
And youthful held the gem-rich citadel.
When Heorogar was dead, my late elder brother,
Halfdane's son, who greater was than I?
470   Then cash settled emnity,
I sent back the Wilfing over sea

Ancient treasures – he swore oaths to me.

'Sore is me to tell to any man
Upon my heart, what Grendel here has done,
475   With deeds unspeakable has ravaged Heorot.
My army is depleted – swept off to their fate
In Grendel's raids. May God's great power
Put an end to this mad slaughterer!
480   Full often at the beer-drinking
Over ale-cups warriors have made vows
That they in the beer-hall would await
Grendel's terror with their swords.
Then was this mead-hall at morning tide,
485   This noble palace bloodstained when day shone,
All the benches steamed with blood,
The hall a shambles. Those I have are less trusty,
Stout veterans were those death took.
Sit now to feasting, and in season meet
490   Glorious victory so whet thy appetite.'
Together then on a beer-hall bench
Were the Geatish men installed,
There the heroes went to sit,
A thane to his duty turned,
495   Ale cups he bore in hand,
Poured the clear brew while the poet sang
Sweetly in Heorot, there were heroes' stories,
The glories of Weder and Dane.

Unferth spoke – Ecglaf's son –
500   That sat at Lord Scyld's foot,
Unbound the battle-rune, was he
Jealous of Beowulf, wished not on earth another man
505   More famous than himself:

'Art thou the Beowulf that with Breca strove
Vain-glorious upon the Sound,
And for fool's boast raced across the deep?
510   Not thee might any man

With love or hatred turn
From thy sorry course.
When thou didst swim the Sound
Wrapped in stream's embrace
Measured the sea strait with cleaving hands
515   Gliding over waves made great
In winter storms. Thou in water's grip
Seven nights did strive,
He beat thee in the Sound,
Had greater strength when in the morning
On Heatho-Raem's the water bore him.
520   Then he sought his homeland dear,
Loved by his countrymen, the Brondings' land,
Fair citadel, where he had folk,
Strongholds and wealth. All his vow with thee
The son of Beanstane faithfully fulfilled.
525   I daresay you'll make a worse bargain
However great a warrior you are,
Fierce fighter, if you dare
Nightlong wait for Grendel's drawing near!'

Beowulf spoke, Ecgtheow's son:

530   'What thou sayest about Breca
My beer-drunken friend Unferth,
Is said from his story. Truth I tell
That I have greater strength, more endurance
On the sea than any other man.

535   When we were boys we did declare
And made vows when still in youth,
That at sea our lives would risk,
And thus did we fulfill that oath:

540   With naked swords hard in our hands
From whales to guard, we swam the Sound,
No whit could he far from me swim
Across the sea, nor I from him.

27

Upon the waves together we
545 Were five nights long, until the sea
Bore us apart in drifting flood,
The rollers welled, the weather cold,
We strove against the wave unkind
In darkening night and northern wind.

A mere-fish stirred in dangerous mood,
550 It came at me! My mail hard,
My hand-locked coat protected me,
Gold-worked upon my breast it lay.
The angry killer dragged me down,
In murderous clutch held fast –
555 Grimly grasped – but Heaven sent
The monster rushing on my sword
And by this onslaught did withstand
The mighty sea-beast through my hand.

Many times the loathsome things
560 Thus pressed me hard, but I served them
My noble sword; they, as was fit,
Not with joy their fill did eat;
The man-eaters received from me
No banquet there beneath the sea,
565 But at morning to me came
Flotsam, washed up by the wave,
The slain-of-sword that never before
Let sailors venture from the shore.

570 'The eastern light, God's beacon bright,
Smoothed the ocean, that I might
See the headland's windy walls;
Courage the undoomed man avails,
Often fortune's favour aids a man of valour.
574 Although it chanced that with my sword
Nine sea-beasts I slew,
I know of no night-battle fought
Harder under heaven's vault,

28

Nor in the waves a man more desperate.
Though far the fierce clutch I endured
Of wearisome ordeal, then me the water upward bore,
580   Flood after foam on Finland's surging shore.

'No whit have I heard from thee
– Such tales of battle under sea –
Of sword-bright danger!
Breca never yet at battle-play –
585   Nor thou either – brave deeds performed this way
With shining blade. I do not boast!
You, though, caused thy brother's deaths,
Close kinsmen. Thus shall you
Get your deserts in hell, for all your wit!
590   I tell thee truly, son of Ecglaf,
That Grendel never would have done these deeds,
These atrocities, humbled thy Prince in Heorot,
If thy courage were at heart as battle-firm
As thyself tellest!
595   But he has found out that he need not fear,
Your people, rather, dread the fierce sword-thrust,
Victorious Scyldings! He takes toll,
600   Spares none of Danish folk,
Sleeps and feasts unfearful of Gardanes.
But I of Geats soon shall show him fight
Hard and glorious. Goes afterward who may
To meadows Valorous, where morning light
605   On sons of men, another day's
Celestial sun, southering, shineth.'

There was in hall one bounteous,
War-famed and grey, counting on aid.
The Danish chieftain heard in Beowulf
610   Steadfast intent.
There was gay laughter, joyous noise,
*   Words were kindly, came Wealtheow forth,
Hrothgar's queen of gentle birth,
Gold-clad to greet the guest in hall.

29

615 And when the gracious lady gave
First the full cup to the East Danes' chief,
She bade him merry at that beer-drinking,
By his people loved. He lustily took
Of feasting and drinking, renowned king.
620 The Lady Helming went round to everyone –
Youth and veteran – with the precious cup.
Till came time that the jewelled queen
Brought Beowulf the cup with gracious mein,
625 Greeted the Geatish Lord, thanked God
In words of wisdom that His will brought
An earl upon whose aid she did rely.
He took the cup, the warrior fierce,
630 At Wealtheow's hand, and then made oath before the fight;

Beowulf spoke, the son of Ecgtheow:

'I that resolved, when on the sea
I set ship with my company,
That I would do unfailingly
635 Your people's will, or fall
Dead in the foe's fast grip. I shall
Fight worthily, or end my days
In this mead-hall, my resting-place.'

Well the Lady liked these words, the Geat's vow;
She went to sit beside her lord,
640 The lovely Queen adorned with gold.

Thereafter was as earlier in hall,
Brave talk of warriors in joyful noise,
645 Until the son of Halfdane all at once
Sought night's repose; he knew
That the monster planned to raid the hall
When sunlight they could see
Sink in darkness over all.
650 From shadow's helm the roving shape
Coming dim beneath the sky.

The warriors all rose,
Then greeted one the other, Hrothgar, Beowulf,
Surrendered him the hall and these words quoth:

655   'I have never, since I carried arms,
Entrusted to another man
The honoured hall of Danes until thee now!
Have now and hold this noblest house,
Be mindful of glory, make valour known,
660   Watch for the enemy.
Be thou not lacking in expectations
If ever thou completest that great task.'

Then Hrothgar left him. With his court
Went Scylding out of hall.
The warrior chief would seek the bed
665   Of Wealtheow the Queen.
The wonder-king, so men were told
Had a hall-guard set holding special ward
Against Grendel, a giant kept guard
By the noble Dane.

670   But with all his heart the Geatish prince
Trusted valour and God's grace
When he put off the shining mail
And gave his serving man his helm,
His ornate sword of choicest iron
To keep for him. Some resolute words
675   Spoke brave Beowulf of Geat
Before he on the bed lay down:

'I count not my courage less than Grendel his,
Therefore with sword I shall not take his life –
680   Though I could with ease. Not so noble he
That he, against me striking, sever shield,
Though he be high in deeds of villainy.
But we shall forego our swords this night,
If he dare seek them, over weapons fight,

31

685   And thence Almighty God on either hand
              Judge the victory as He thinks right.'

              Then brave his head on the bolster laid,
              And round him many a bold comrade
690   At rest in hall. Inwardly none of them thought
              To see his dear homeland again,
              His people or the fair hamlet
              Where he was born.
695   For they'd heard of the wine-hall killer
              That carried off many a Dane,
              But God granted victory's mantle
              Supported the Wederer men,
              To prosper and aid one alone
              That stoutly the foe overcame,
700   For truly is known the Almighty
              Governs the spirit of man.

              Dim in the dark came the roving shape,
              The warriors slept that held the hall -
705   All but one. It was known to men
              That he could not when God willed it not
              Be by the killer dragged beneath the shades,
              But he watched for the foe alone –
              Awaited with beating heart the reckoning.

710   Then came Grendel from the mist-clad moor,
              God's wrath defying, the murderer meant
              To trap some men in the towering hall.
              Went under stars to where the house -
715   The rich hall of warriors, bright with gold,
              Lavishly shone. No first time was that
              That he sought Hrothgar's home.
              Never in bygone days before or since
              Found he hall-thanes tougher in defence.

720   Came then to Heorot the soul-bereft, the roving one.
              At once he rushed the door.

Iron hinges held until
He wrenched them with his hands undone,
Stood then on the gaping sill
The frenzied slaughterer.
725 Swiftly trod the tiled floor,
In fury went, his staring eyes
Glaring with uncanny light,
A warrior band in the wine-hall saw
In comradeship together slept.
730 Laughed to himself the murderer,
The life of each he meant to take
To feast his fill before day break.

735 It was not destined that he might
Slay men again beyond that night.

Steadily Hygelac's kinsman watched.
How would the foe fare under attack?
Not that the monster thought to delay
740 But swiftly seized upon the first:
Slashed the sleeper unaware, gorged great gobbets,
Slavered gore. The lifeless corpse
745 He soon devoured complete – hand and foot.

Stepping near, seized then in hand
The brave warrior as he lay,
With fiendish paw did stretch...
Swift he grabbed the evil-doer
And set upon the wretch.
750 At once the devil's henchman found
That in all corners of the land
He had not met in any man
A greater grasp. His courage failed,
His heart afraid could not retreat,
755 His spirit in defeat would flee
Safety seeking, demon company,
Nor was his ordeal there
As he had met in all his days before.

Then Hygelac's gallant cousin
Fulfilled his evening speach:
Upright stood and fast him grappled,
760   The giant, fingers bursting, struggled.
The earl stepped forth on victory bent
Before he might twist free and thence
Flee on the track to the lair in the fen.
765   His fingers felt power in the terrible grasp,
Unhappy the hour that had drawn him to Heorot,
The wine-hall dinned. (All the Danes had become
Castle-dwellers, keener each one,
Earls, upon ale-sharing).
Both combatants in fury raged, the building rang.

770   Great wonder then
The hall contained the struggling men,
The mansion fair did not collapse,
But out and in it was that fast –
775   Cunning with iron bands was braced.
In that rich wine-hall I have heard
Many a mead bench wrought with gold
Was torn from its sill in contest grim.
Wise Scyldings knew it no man's lot
780   To wreck the fine mansion, ivory-wrought,
No art could tear it down unless
Wrapped by flame in fire's embrace.

The din rose up, furiously renewed,
Terror-struck the North Danes stood,
Each one a surge of anguish heard –
785   A ghastly howl beyond the wall.
God's enemy surrender sang,
The slave of hell had shrieked with pain,
Held him fast the strongest one
790   In all those days of living men.

The earl would not by any means

Allow the fiend escape alive,
Nor count his life of use in any land.
795 All Beowulf's warriors drew their swords
And would defend their brave lord's life
As best they might. They did not know
When they joined battle, loyal followers,
800 And thought to hew in half the murderer,
The the choicest iron on earth
Could not affect the evil-doer.
But victory's weapon – every sword –
805 Beowulf had forsworn, should his rich share
Of this life's days run low,
And he an outcast spirit far
In the realms of demons go.

Then found the savage, who had once
810 Rejoiced his mind in cruelty to men
And fought with God, he could not win.
But Hygelac's valiant kinsman had him by the hand,
815 Each faced the other in mortal hate;
A fatal wound the cannibal sustained,
For in his shoulder clearly seen
Sinews unsprung, bursting flesh
The victory was Beowulf's.
Then did Grendel, wounded mortally,
820 Flee to the rolling fen to seek his joyless home,
Knowing for sure that his life's end was come –
Numbered, his days.
The goal of all the Danes had been achieved,
825 Hrothgar's hall was cleansed,
Saved by one who came from far,
Joyful night's work, glorious deed!
The Geat's vow to the East Danes thus fulfilled,
830 Their every grief assuaged, their sorrows borne,
Their not little sufferings endured.
Clear the proof, for the murdering hand,
835 Arm and shoulder – all Grendel's grasp –
Lay under the vaulted roof.

In the morning I have heard
Many warriors gathered there,
Leaders travelled far and near
840   Along the roads, in wonder gazing
On the relic of the foe.
His life's ending caused no sorrow
To them that saw his vanquished tracks,
How he wearied on the way
Overcome by agony;

845   The surface of the demon mere
Doomed and fleeing life-blood bore,
Horribly the wavelets swirled
All mingled with hot gore;
The spreading stains of war
Death's fated one concealed;
850   Thence comfortless within the fen
His life the heathen soul laid down,
Hell took him then.

Then soon returned the old retainers
And youths who many joyful journeys
855   Rode from the mere, brave on their steeds.
There Beowulf's glory was proclaimed,
Many declared that, south or north,
860   Under heaven or on wide earth,
By seas between, none other was
Better than he, nor greater worth.
Nor did they their lord one whit rebuke,
Gracious Hrothgar, but - that king was good.

*   At times they let their horses race
865   In contest on the yellow mares
Where roads were fair from custom's use;
At times the king's thane, story-laden,
Mindful of history, the man
Who all the many tales of old recalled,
870   Found other words the truth to bind,

The story to pass on of Beowulf's feat.
His cunning stirred, and speedily the news he framed
In aptly chosen words. Told everything
875 *   That he of Sigemund's story heard,
Courageous deeds extraordinary,
The Waelsing's wars wide ranging,
Conflict and feud unknown to men,
None but Fitela with him
880   To whom he would recount somewhat,
Uncle to nephew, as they were aye
Comrades in adversity; many of giants' race
Had their swords felled. Sigemund sprang
885   After his death to greatest fame:
For that warrior overpowered
A serpent, guardian of a hoard:
He beneath an ancient stone,
Son of princes, went alone,
Deed of terror! Fitela
Wasn't with him then.
890   Chance gave that his sword ran through
The artful-fashioned worm:
There from the wall was sticking out
The noble iron.
Murderous, the serpent died,
The monster surely gone
That he might broach the treasure hoard
895   For himself to claim.
Laden the ship whose bosom bore
*   Bright wealth of Wael's son.
The worm – heat melted down.

*   He was of warriors most widely famed,
Over nations, a chieftain of great deeds.
900   Thus once he thrived. Then Heremod's war
Diminished enterprise and honour: Sigemund
Among the Eoten was betrayed in power of foes,
905   Soon put to death. Remorse lamed Heremod too long,
He to his people, all his noblemen, became

37

Too great a shame. Often they mourned
The hero's venturing of former time;
Many a man of sense believed
To repay his wickedness,
910   That that prince's son should rise,
Sieze his father's title, rule the folk,
Hoard and citadel, champion the realm
Of Scyldings, where Hygelac's kinsman
Was to all their dearest friend.
915   Madness possessed Heremod.

While ponies raced the fallow street,
Morning light moved on in haste,
Came many warriors to that high hall
920   The trophy to see. The king himself
The treasurer, went from his chamber,
Well-renowned, followed by his train,
And with him on the meadow path
Amid her troop of maids, his Queen.
925   Hrothgar spoke – he to hall going,
Stood at the stay-pole, saw the steep roof
Wrought with gold, and Grendel's hand.

'For this sight at once be thanks to God!
Great bitterness have I endured at Grendel's hand,
930   Ever may God work wonder after wonder –
Shepherd of miracles! That lately was
That I daren't hope that any, far or wide,
Might bring redress. The bloodstained royal house
935   Horror-dreary stood midst woe widespread;
Councillors all did not believe
That ever could stout hearts defend
This fort from devils and from wizardry.
940   Now has a warrior through God's power
Performed the deed that we before could not
With all skill contrive.

What can each tribe tell to equal that?

As a mother knows of a son conceived –
If yet she lives – that God's Grace
945 Was with her at his birth
Now I, Beowulf, thee, noblest of men,
Will in spirit love before my son,
Hold henceforth in new relationship.
Nor shalt thou lack in this world anything
950 That I have power to give.
Oft have I rewarded smaller enterprise –
Lesser men with treasure honouring –
Feebler warriors. Thou hast thyself
A deed performed that liveth thine –
955 Great for ever more.
God reward thee as he did just now!'

Beowulf spoke, the son of Ecgtheow:
'We, that much esteem a noble task,
960 Brought the fight to pass, rashly risked ordeal unknown.
Rather I wish that thou couldst have seen himself –
The foe fill-weary in his ornaments.
Suddenly I gripped him hard,
Writhing on the bed of death,
965 Meant that he within my grasp should lay down life.
Bar his escape I could not,
For God would not prevent his going,
Not eagerly I hugged him thus in deadly strife;
Too strong afoot the devil was,
970 But he left his paw to save his life,
Arm and shoulder followed; poor men nowhere
Prosper at that price. The hated one
Will not live long, burdened with crime,
975 But hath a wound whose grip surrounds him close
In bonds of death, where he shall bide
Sin-stained his doom
As enlightened Justice will decide.'

980 Then was the swordsman quieter, Ecglaf's son,
In boast of battle-prowess, since the chiefs

Over the high roof gazed on earl's work –
The hand, the fingers of the foe.
985 Before each one instead of nails
A heathen claw like steel was –
A talon harsh; all declared
That finest iron of warriors could not injure him,
990 That this monstrous bloody battle-paw would overwhelm.

Then soon were ordered hands to decorate
Heorot within; many there were
Of men and wives who decked that house,
Servants in hall; gold-bright shone
995 Tapestry upon the wall, sights wonderful
To every man who gazed thereon.
Greatly damaged was that noble room,
All its iron-fast bonds within
Were fiercely wrenched, the roof alone
1000 Remained quite sound; the savage, struggling
To flee in life's despair, this damage did;
It is not easy to escape - do so who will -
1005 But human beings shall seek, their needs compelling
Ever the sons of men upon earth dwelling
A place where the body, safe in the grave,
Sleeps after feasting.

Then was time and season
That to hall went Halfdane's son,
1010 The king himself to feast would come.
No court I heard of bore themselves
So well before their bounteous lord,
At the benches sat them down,
Contented and pleased, fairly to take
1015 Many cups of mead, kinsmen of those
Heroes in hall, those noblemen
* Hrothgar and Hrothwulf; within was Heorot
With friendship filled, no treachery yet
Was planned by lords of Scyld.

40

1020   They gave Beowulf Halfdane's brand,
            A golden emblem in reward,
            Ornamental banner, arms and helm.
            Many saw the famous jewelled sword
            As it was brought before the champion.
1025   Beowulf's riches filled the floor,
            Not slighted he before his men,
            Nor heard I four more precious treasures
            Adorned with gold that anyone
            Gave at the mead-bench to another.
1030   Round the helmet's crown a guard
            Of wire winding held the outer rim
            That no blade might injure him
            Should foe oppose the veteran.

1035   Eight horses then the king ordained
            With golden-plated bridles, led
            Into the court, on one of them
            An ornate war-seat, gem-rich stood,
            Saddle of the noble king,
1040   That Scyld used in battle-play –
            Never at the front in war
            Failed the famous warrior.

*   And then every treasure
            The Ingwine's ruler gave
1045   To Beowulf, horse and weapon,
            'Use them well' he bade
            So manfully the famous prince,
            Stout guardian of the hoard,
            With horses and with riches
            Brave battles did reward,
            That never man in him found fault
            Who told the story true and right.

1050   Then each of the earl's following yet –
            They that were with him on the voyage –
            At the mead-bench were enriched

41

With heirlooms and precious gifts;
Then was commanded to give gold
For the one that Grendel's crime had slain,
1055 As more of them he would, but God
All-knowing, had their fate withstood,
And one man's bravery.
God ruled all men as he does yet now,
Thus highest understanding everywhere
1060 Is a thankful spirit. Shall endure
Much of love and hatred, he who here
Long partakes of this world's troubled days.

There was music and song; in unison
1065 Harps greeted Halfdane's foremost captains;
Hrothgar's scop – hall-poet – often made
Histories at the mead-bench to relate:
* 'When battle seized the sons of Finn,
The Halfdane chief, Hnaef Scylding,
1070 In Friesian war must fall.
No good cause had Hildeburh
The Jutes' good troth to laud,
Guiltless she of love was lorn
Upon that battle-ground –
Son and brother born to die
1075 Of spear's swift wound.
Sorrowful, that lady
Not for nothing Fate bewailed,
When morning came the slaughter
Under heaven was revealed
Of the loved ones that Hoc's daughter
Held most dear in all the word.

1080 War took all Finn's warriors
Except a few alone,
Thus could he not in battle
A whit Hengest overcome,
Nor the royal thane's survivors
By warfare overwhelm.

1085   But they with them made compact
           That they cleared another floor,
           Hall and throne, to share the rule
           With Jutes' sons as their own.
1090   And each day the son of Folcwald,
           At paying of Danes, must treat
           Hengest's men to precious rings –
           Equal gold they would expect
           In the beer-hall as his Friesian men received.

1095   Then they swore on both sides
           That they were fast as one,
           Finn Hengest honour's witness
           To an oath did name:
           That he would hold in council
           The survivors in easteem,
           That it would not be broken
1100   Word or deed by any man;
           Nor through hatred ever –
           Though they their leader's killer,
           Leaderless, must follow –
           The Danes must not complain:

           Forced by need, thus, he must give
           To Friesians, any one
1105   Daring to recall the feud
           The sword's edge thereupon.

           The oath was sealed, and gold withal
           Drawn from out the hoard. Was bounteous
           Lord Scylding prepared for funeral;
1110   At the pyre was plainly seen
           The bloodstained mail, the golden swine –
           Iron-hard – the Boar;
           Many brave men of mortal wounds
           Had perished in that war.

           Then Hildeburh commended

1115 At Hnaef's pyre, her son,
Her child's body to the flames
Shoulders bowed, she mourned,
Sorrowful the lady, sad the song.
Up rose the warrior with the great death fire
1120 Darkening the heavens, heralding the grave,
Brains moulten, wounds bursting,
Blood springing, death stinging,
Flames swallowed all.
Avid, the spirit of war did wrest
From every tribe the bravest, best.
1125 Warriors returning visited their homes,
Friends dispersed – Friesland to see,
Hamlets and towns.
Hengest yet one war-stained winter
Stayed with Finn in equal honour,
1130 Held his ground, although might he
Ring-prowed have sailed over sea.
The storm-swollen ocean
Strove with the winds – waves winter-locked
1135 In icy bonds. So in completion another year passed
As now it doth yet, when weather gently bright
The enduring skies await.

When winter was shaken from earth's fair bosom,
Hastened the traveller, guest, from the court;
He to wreak vengeance thought, rather than sea-going,
1140 If the encounter he might bring about
That he inwardly purposed, son of the Jutes.

Thus he did not reject ancient traditions
Which Hunlafing, war-shining, urged in his breast
1145 (Noblest of blades this was, famed among giants).
Thus fierce-hearted Finn later incurred
Death by sword swiftly in his own abode,
When the grim raiders Guthlaf and Oslaf
1150 Returned from their sea-trip, sorrow and grief
Couldn't hinder the wanderers' rage in its speed:

44

Then was hall strewn with the bodies of dead.

Suchwise Finn slain in the midst of his followers,
His queen carried off, and the Scylding warriors
1155   Took away to their ship all the earth-king's possessions,
All they could find of jewels and gems;
From Finn's home forth upon the sea laden,
Brought they to her homeland the Queen to the Danes.

1160   The lay was sung, the gleeman's song.
With noise and music benches rang.
Wine was brought in marvellous vessels,
Forth came Wealtheow, laden with jewels,
And the good twain, each to each true,
Sat yet at peace – uncle and nephew.
1165   Likewise Unferth, spokesman, sat
At Lord Scyld's foot; all trusted at heart
That he was brave, though never he
Avenged his kinsmen at battle-play.
Then spoke the Scylding's Lady;

'Receive this cup, my noble, gracious lord,
1170   Be thou duly generous to the men,
And to the Geats speak kindly word
As a man should do, be liberal with them,
Remember the treasures that now you have
1175   Near and far. Men tell me thou
Wouldst hold the warrior before thy son.
Heorot is made clean, the treasure-hall,
Then make use of many rewards
And to thy Kinsmen leave folk and realm
1180   When forth thou shalt meet thy God.
I know my gracious Hrothwulf that he will
In honour hold our youngsters if do thou,
Lord Scyld, before him leave this world.
With good he will repay them I believe
1185   If he remembers all that we
Willing have done and honourably

45

Of kindness when he was a boy'.

She turned to the bench where her children were,
Hrethric and Hrothmund, warrior's sons,
1190   The young men together, and honoured sat
Beowulf of Geat between the brothers.
To him the cup was brought and offered
With gracious words and presents given
Of twisted gold: two bracelets,
1195   Corselet and rings, a jewelled collar
The best on earth of which I know

*   None better under skies I heard
From heroes' hoards, since Hama brought
The Brosing necklace to the war-bright fort,
1200   Jewels and gems; fled Eormanric's armed warriors
Greater Council chose.
That ring had Hygelac of the Geats,
*   Swerting's descendant, his last exploit,
For when he under banners defended the treasure,
1205   The war-spoil of warriors, fate him destroyed
When he in vain-glory sought to make war,
To feud with the Friesians, that jewel he wore
The precious stones over the very waves,
Prince of the realm; he fell under shield,
1210   Passed the king's corpse
Then into power of the Franks,
His breast-plate and this jewel too;
Worse warriors rifled the bodies,
After war's carnage the Geatish tribe
Nought but a grave-yard occupied.

There was music in hall,
1215   Wealtheow made speach, said before all:
'Accept, Beowulf, these gifts of love,
Brave young man, and these trappings use –
A nation's treasure – and prosper well!
Daring, thou, and skillful, and to these boys

1220 Be a gentle tutor; I shall requite thee.
Thou hast ensured that ever far and near
Thy great courage warriors praise –
Even where ocean's widest bounds,
The home of surging winds, surrounds.
1225 Be, while you live, nobleman, fortunate!
I grant thee fit reward, be to my sons
Thou in loyal deeds a trusty friend.
'Here each earl is to the other true,
Kind thoughts the warriors think,
1230 Thanes are as one, the land united,
Those do as I entreat – who drink.'

Went she to the high seat; choice was the feast,
Warriors drank wine, their fate unknowing –
1235 The grim decree as dealt to many a man;
Till evening came and to his room
Went Hrothgar – ruler – to his rest.
In the hall stayed countless earls
As they often had before: clearing the benches
1240 There they spread bolster and bed.
Of these revellers, one fated and doomed
To rest lay down. At their heads
The shields set – bright-wood boards – upon a bench
Above the nobles plainly seen
1245 The war-steep helm, the mail ringed,
The mighty spear. Their custom was
That they often kept one soldier armed
Whether at home or whether on campaign,
Or any time their lord had need of them,
1250 These people were prepared.

They fell asleep: one paid sore
For that night's rest, as oft before
When to the gold hall Grendel came
With dire intention, till he met his end –
1255 Death after sin.
It was seen – men knew clear

That an avenger was yet there,
Alive from the fight long, wretched
After bitter war; Grendel's mother
Woman, troll's wife, knew the curse
1260 Who should dwell in the water fierce
The currents cold, since ever Cain
His own brother's slayer became –
His father's son. He bore that stain,
The murderer's mark, outcast from men,
1265 The wilderness to roam; thence awoke
Many damned spirits whereof was Grendel one,
The horror-hateful foe who found at Heorot
A watchful warrior awaiting war.
The errant one attacked him there,
1270 But he remembered his great power
The precious gift God gave,
And he in Almighty God believed,
To succour and sustain;
Therefore he overcame the foe,
Laid the hell-fiend low, that joyless went
1275 Defeated to his place of death,
The enemy of men; and his mother then,
Avid yet and sad at heart, would go
A son's death to avenge, journey in sorrow.

Came then to Heorot, where Ring Danes
1280 Slept around the room; then for earls
Was swift reverse when entered Grendel's dam.
Was this lesser terror even so
Great as is the strength, the skill of amazons
Alongside men when harnessed to the blade:
1285 Hammer-forged the edge-hard sword
With blood the severed boar-crest stains
Above opposing helms.
Then in hall was drawn the tempered blade,
1290 The sword before the throne, and fast in hand
Were many broad shields raised, none cared for helm
Nor armour stout, when they the danger understood.

She was in haste to get from thence
Safely afar, before she was perceived,
Then quickly one of noble blood she siezed
1295 In fast embrace, and onward to the fen.
It was Hrothgar's dearest thane
Of noble birth between the seas,
Fine shield-man, the one she grasped
As he lay at rest – most famous, best.
1300 Beowulf was not there, but other rooms
Assigned in honour, when valiant Geats
Were given treasure.

There was uproar in Heorot.
She took the famous bloody hand,
Grief again came on the land,
1305 No fair exchange was this, that double they must pay
In comrades dead. Then was the aged king,
The old soldier, sad in mind
For his departed noble thane,
Knowing the death of his dear friend.

1310 In haste victorious Beowulf
Was summoned to the throne,
The warrior went ere daybreak
To attend the wise old man,
Wondering when Almighty God
1315 Would send good tidings after bad.
Marching then across the floor
The wood resounding dinned,
The hero went amidst his men:
That in his manner, the Lord Ingwin
Subdued enquiring words – if him
1320 At this sudden call, the night had pleased?

Hrothgar spoke, the Lord of Scyldings:

'Ask not thou after pleasure.
Disaster is repeated on the Danes.

49

Dead is Aeschere, Yrmenlaf's elder brother,
1325 My adviser and my staff-bearer,
Comrade at my shoulder
When we in battle headed the assault
And clashed against opposing boar-crests;
As earls should be – the best –
So Aeschere was.
1330 On him in Heorot the slayer's hand,
Death's errant spirit, did descend;
Unknown where, carrion-fed, the ghoul
Has hid the corpse, her frightful meal;
But she this injury has wrought
That thou didst Grendel slay last night
1335 In furious hold didst wrench him hard
Who had too long my nation harried;
He, out-fought, fell ever damned,
And now another murderer comes
That her kinsman would avenge;
1340 Yet further drags vendetta on
For many followers of this thane
In mind bewail their bounteous one
With heavy hearts – low lies the hand
Now, that did once your needs command.'

1345 'At the councils of the nation
I have heard the folk declare
That they have seen upon the marches
Such a giant pair – border-roving
Outcast spirits hold the moor.
Of them was one in woman's likeness
1350 As most sure they told,
'The other, misshaped, in warrior's form
Trod the exile's road;
Giant he was among all men,
The one in yore days 'Grendel' named
by countrymen.
1355 Unknown his sire, if such he ever had,
Of spirits dire mysteriously bred.

50

These people dwell in hidden lands,
Wolf-haunted slopes and windy capes,
A mountain stream led through the fen
1360 There under misty crag runs down,
The flood below the ground.
Not far from hence in miles marked
That mere stands; frost-rinded boughs
Above it hang, whose stubborn roots
1365 The water overwhelms. There at night have men
A fiendish wonder seen – fire in the flood!
No man living knows the depth.
Though the stag, hard-pressed by hound,
The antlered hart does thicket's refuge seek,
Far pursued, he sooner yields his life –
1370 Dies on the shore ere he in there will head.
That is no pleasant place
Where spray up-flung wars with the sky
Stirred by the wind in storm so dread
1375 That heaven, weeping, drowns the air.

'Now help depends on thee alone,
Knowest not yet the frightful den
Where you may find the evil one -
Seek if you dare!
For this feat I shall reward you
Richest treasure as before
Of winding gold, if you return from there.'

Said Beowulf, Ecgtheow's son:

'Grieve not, wise one! Better for man
1385 That he avenge his friend than mourn;
To each the end must come of this world's life,
The best die seeking high renown.
1390 Arise, Protector of the Realm,
Let's be on our way
Tracks of Grendel's kin to see –
I promise you he shall not flee

Not in thicket nor beneath the sea,
1395   Go where he will, this day thou hast
All sorrows passed – so I believe of thee!'

Then arose the veteran
Thanked God, Almighty Lord,
For this man's words.
Then Hrothgar's horse was bitted,
1400   The steed with plaited mane,
Splendid went the chieftain,
Men on foot bore shields.
Tracks along the forest path
Across the ground were clearly seen
1405   Going straight for the misty moor,
Where she, of all in Hrothgar's home,
His noblest subject, dying, bore.

Over rocky hillsides steep
That brave nobleman went up
The stoney defile closed,
1410   The unknown pathway narrowing
Past rocks that demon spirits housed.
He with few that went before,
Wise men to scan the ground,
Came suddenly where the mountain trees
1415   Over a weathered boulder leaned
And underneath the water stood,
Stirred about and stained with blood.

All Scyld's Danish following
Horror and woe knew there,
To each the grief of many men
1420   For on that cliff they came upon
The head of Aeschere!
Blood swelled the flood for folk to see,
Not yet cold, the gore.

Sounded the horn in urgent song,

                  All the soldiers, crouching down,
1425   Into the water peered
                  (Strange sea-dragons, serpents vile
                  In such upland waters crawl
                  Which in broad day-light often wait
                  For rash adventurers in the lake –
1430   Wild beast and water-snake,
                  They the clarion understood,
                  Drew away in bitter mood,
                  The war-horn calling).

                  Some creature by the Geatish Lord
                  Of a distant bow-shot stricken,
                  Struggled in the mere.
1435   In its vitals stood the boult
                  As it swam with slowing stroke
                  Borne by death away.
                  Soon was hard-pressed in the water
                  Amidst boar-spears hooked with horror,
1440   By men attacked, the wierd wave-borer,
                  And dragged to land.
                  Soldiers examined the gruesome catch.

                  In armour Beowulf girded him,
                  He did never danger fear,
                  Putting on the hand-locked mail
                  Sear and stout, to scan the deep,
1445   To be the body's tested shield
                  That his breast no clutch of war,
                  No malicious thrust might tear;
                  But that shining helm he wore
                  Who should scan the bottom of the mere,
1450   The swirling waters in costly gear,
                  Wearing the chain that in olden time
                  The weapon-smith worked with magic sign,
                  Set with likeness of the swine,
                  Not to be broke by sword or brand.
1455   Not the least of powerful aid

                                          53

Him Hrothgar's spokesman lent at need
Was Hrunting named, the hilted sword
Of ancient heirlooms this most froward,
The iron blade with poison stained
1460   Hardened in war, had never failed
Any man whose hand encircled it,
Who perilous deeds dared undertake
To a foeman's home; no first time this
That it should gain a victory.
1465   For Ecglaf's kinsman remembered not
What he, wine-drunken, said before
When, strong and able, he lent this weapon
To a nobler swordsman; himself dared not
Risk his life beneath the water,
1470   Undergo danger, there he missed
His chance of high renown. Not so the other,
He had prepared himself for war.

Beowulf spoke, the son of Ecgtheow:

'Great son of Halfdane, honoured chief,
1475   I am now ready for this task.
Think now, dear friend, of what we said –
If at thy need I life must give,
That thou to me wert held for ever
In death departing, as a father.
1480   Be thou protector of my thanes,
My comrades true, if me war claims;
Such presents you to me have given,
Dear Hrothgar, send to Hygelac on.
When the measure of that gold
Is known to the Geatish Lord –
When that wealth he looks upon
1485   Hrethel's son will understand
That I a great and good lord found,
A bounteous chieftain must have known.
And thou let Unferth have the heirloom,
The patterned blade famous to men,

1490   With Hrunting I shall work my fate,
              Or take me, death.'

              After these words the Wedergeat Lord
              With eager haste no answer would bide;
              The surging wave closed over him then,
1495   A day's while passed ere he saw the plain.

              Soon found the savage, avid and grim
              Who fifty years that river country held,
1500   That from above some man the place explored;
              Grappling then, the atrocious claws
              Siezed the warrior; they never cut through
              To the body whole – his outer mail
              Close covered him, armour that could not be rent,
1505   Fingers tore at the chain-locked coat.

              The water's surge so bore them
              That they to the bottom came,
              The mailed chieftain to her den.
              Thus no weapon could he wield
              Though none so brave as he,
1510   But him so many monsters
              Assailed in the depths,
              Many a toothed sea-creature
              Broke the mail the giant attacked.
              Then the earl perceived
              That he in a sort of dwelling was,
1515   Where, for the height, the water's grip
              Could reach to harm him not a whit,
              Fire-light he saw gleaming bright
              In the darkness shone.

              When the warrior saw the cavern ogress,
              The mighty mere-wife, his sword raced,
1520   Nor did his hand its onrush stay
              Till on her head the arching blade
              Clanged an eager battle-lay.

The blade failed.
At his need the invader found
The gleaming weapon could not wound.
1525 Many encounters had it known –
Fights hand-to-hand endured,
Many a fair corselet and helm
Had that bright treasure sheared;
This the first adventure was
In which its glory made it false.
1530 Still resolute, his eagerness undimmed,
Hygelac's cousin on valour determined
Angrily dropped the wave-patterned sword,
It lay on the ground, taut steel blade.

Trusting the strength of his bare hands,
As a man shall do who thinks to gain
1535 In the battle lasting fame, reckless of life,
He siezed by the shoulder Grendel's dam.
Not fearing a battle the war–Geat Lord
Invited then a struggle hard,
1540 Furious, his foe, borne to the earth,
Swift replied with a countergrasp.
Then Weariness, war's strongest soldier,
Filled him overwhelmingly.
1545 She straddled him and drew her knife –
Broad Bright-Edge would her only child avenge!
Lay on his shoulders the woven coat,
The blade it barred, the point withstood.

1550 Ecgtheow's son had perished then
Trapped under ground, the Geatish thane,
Had not his armour aided him,
The war-net hard, and holy God
Sent victory. The Lord all-wise,
1555 The heavenly Judge, decided the law with ease,
And he arose.
* Then he saw as he fought a triumphant blade,
A gigantic old sword of powerful edge

56

Honoured by warriors; choice, that weapon,
1560   Though it was more than any other man could do
To bear it in the fray,
Good and well-fashioned, a giant work.
Scyld's avenger siezed the ringed hilt,
Drew, grim and enraged, a fatal arc,
1565   Of life despairing furiously swept –
Hard gashed the blade against her neck,
Broke the bones, severed the fated flesh,
She fell to the floor. Bloody the sword,
The swordsman rejoiced.

1570   The luminous glow, the inward light stood
Just as heaven's bright candle shines.
He next faced the cavern, moved by the wall,
Holding the weapon hard by the hilt,
1575   Hygelac's thane, tense and alert.
Not useless so, the warrior's sword,
For he would Grendel soon reward
For many raids upon the Danes,
Above all for a certain occasion when
1580   Of Hrothgar's hearth-thanes, sleeping, slain,
Fifteen Danish men devoured
And carried off as many more.
This the fearless champion
Had so rewarded that he found
1585   At rest war-weary Grendel lying
Lifeless from his earlier wound
At the fight in Heorot. The body gaped
From the death-blow he had suffered.
1590   The sword swung hard and cut his head off.

Soon the wise companions saw,
Who with Hrothgar scanned the mere,
That the white water was all streaked –
The wave was stained with blood.
1595   Grey-haired veterans conferred,
Guessed that now this noble chief

57

Would not return to the royal prince;
Most were sure that he'd been killed
By the she-wolf of the mere.
1600 Came day's ninth hour. The Scyldings bold
Abandoned then the cliff; thence went he home,
True friend of men. The strangers searching on
Sick at heart gazed on the mere,
Longing, without hope, to see
1605 Their dear lord himself.
Then that sword, the blade
Blood-icicled from battle stain,
Began to wane. That marvel was
That it melted all, like ice;
The bond of frost the Father looseneth
1610 Unwinds the shroud of death;
He that power of time and season hath,
That is the God of Truth.

He took not from their dwelling,
The Weder-Geatish Lord,
A more valuable possession –
Though many there he saw –
Than the head and hilt together,
1615 Jewelled treasure.
The blade had crumbled earlier,
Its pattern all consumed,
Was the blood of that strange Being
So poisonous that it died therein.

Soon was in the water he
Who before had lived to see
The enemy's defeat;
Upward through the river plunged,
1620 All the turmoiled wave was cleansed,
The mighty den, when its ghastly inmate
Relinquished life and paid the debt.

Came then to land the sailors' captain,

	Pleased with his loot, valiantly swimming,
1625	Weighty the burden that with him he had.
	Thanking God the loyal thanes approached,
	Overjoyed to see their leader sound,
	Quickly the stout helm and corselet loosed;
1630	Beneath the sky the blood-stained water drowsed.

	They set forth on the path in happy mood,
	The little track a well-known street,
1635	Bold as kings from the cliff the trophy bore,
	Each one upon the task determined more -
	Four must carry to the golden hall
	Upon their spears the head of Grendel.
1640	Till presently to the hall they came,
	Vigorous and war-like, the fourteen
	Geatish men with their fine chief,
	In gallant company the meadows trod.

	When they arrived the leader went –
1645	The man of action, proved by fate
	Fearless in war – Hrothgar to greet.
	Then by its hair across the floor
	Where men drank, the head they bore,
	Ghastly before the earls and ladies,
1650	All looked upon the frightful visage.

Said Beowulf, the son of Ecgtheow:

	'Son of Halfdane, what we bring
	With pleasure to Lord Scylding –
	Sea–plunder for souvenir –
	That thou seest here!
1655	I, that scarce with life survived
	War under waves, did undertake
	A heavy task – was dead outright
	Unless God shielded me.
	Nor could I do a whit
1660	With Hrunting in the fight

59

(though a fine weapon, that)
But the Almighty granted me
That I saw hanging on the wall
A huge old sword (most often He
Guides those bereft of friends)
When I swung that weapon,
Then, in war cut down,
1665   Occasion yielded me
The keeper of the den.
Then that war-bill, the patterned blade
Dissolved as the blood sprang hot –
The sweat of death.
Thence from the foe the hilt I carried off,
1670   Dreadful wrongs avenged, the murdering of Danes,
As was fit.
I promised thee that thou in Heorot must sleep
Sorrowless, amidst thy thanes and folk,
That thou needst not fear for old and young
1675   Lord Scyld, on their behalf, as once thou didst.'
Then was the golden hilt of ancient men
Into the hand of that grey warrior given,
Work of by-gone giants, it passed into the power,
1680   After the fiend's death, of the Danish ruler,
He quit this world – God's foe,
Murder-guilty, and his mother too,
It passed into the earthly king's possession
1685   The best by seas between
That treasure shared in Scane.

Hrothgar spoke, examining the ancient relic's hilt,
Was carved on it the origins, the early wars,
Then flood destroyed in deluge sent
1690   The giants' race, a frightful happening,
That was done by eternal God, the Lord sent them
Retribution thus through water's whelm.
So was on the sword-guard clear in gold
1695   By rune-staves rightly marked, set out and told
For whom that sword was made at first

60

In iron choice, the spiralled hilt
And serpent ornament.

Then spoke the son of Halfdane,
All were still:

1700   'That tale he may recite who in the nation
Truth and law does frame
(Far back in time old Ethelward recalls)
That this earl was born most great!
Beowulf, my friend, thy glory rises
1705   Beyond the wide ways, over every race,
All thy great strength in power and wisdom hold,
I shall honour my debt to thee as first we said;
Thou shalt prosper, to thy people ever
Strong to save!

'Not so was Heremod to Ecgwela's sons,
1710   Lord Scylding, nor thrived he by their will,
But by slaughter and murder of Danish folk.
Suspicious killed his comrades close,
Turned solitary, the famous prince
1715   From all mens' joys.
Though God Almighty had raised him
Great in power above all men,
Yet in heart did he become
A bitter miser, giving none
1720   Of Danes, for services, reward.
Grief prevailed that he thus
Worked through emnity and strife
Long oppression of the land.
Learn thou by that. To virtue cleave.
Wise in years I tell thee this.
1725   Wonder is to say how mighty God
Gives mankind grace through generosity,
Land and earlship, He all power possessing.
Whiles He in love lets come about
Man's thoughts of noble lineage,

61

1730	Raises him highest, earthly joys to hold –
	A citadel to rule – and sets him so
	To govern His wide realm in part,
	That he in his unwisdom can conceive
	No ending to himself.
1735	He lives in plenty, no whit in him
	Old age nor sickness dwell,
	Nor in contention anywhere
	Is hatred's edge displayed,
	But all the world bends to his will.

1740	'He that adversity knows not,
	Or in whom pride in his lot waxes and grows –
	His guardian sleeps.
	Be this sleep too sound, by evil bound,
	A slayer nears who shoots a deadly boult,
1745	One that swiftly strikes beneath the helm,
	A bitter shaft, and no defence has he,
	Commanded by demons of perversity –
	Thinking too little that which he holds too long,
1750	Suspicious, avaricious, bestows no honoured ring,
	And, Destiny forgetting, by Destiny forgot,
	Whom once God in his glory gave so excellent a lot.
	The end comes soon – that this spent body fails,
1755	Falls doomed; another comes
	Who treasure shares ungrudged,
	Heeds not fears for earls' inheritance.

	'Remember that ill-doer, Beowulf, love,
	Best of men, and that higher council choose,
1760	Heed not pride, great champion, now is thine
	Glory for a while; soon after it may be
	That sickness or the knife bring sorrow thee,
1765	Or fire's fang, or flood's whelm,
	Or sword's gripe, or spear's flight,
	Or dotage dread, or the eyes dim
	Fail and wane – sudden be, Chieftain,
	That death cuts thee down.

'So the Ringdanes under heaven
1770   Half a hundred winters I did govern,
And, of mind for war, did lock
With many a foeman spear and sword,
Till I could count in all the world
No adversary under God.

'What a change upon me came –
Grief after joy upon my home,
1775   When Grendel, long my enemy,
Invaded mine. I knew great care
Harrassed by continuing war.
God of victory and law be thanked
For this that I have waited long to see,
1780   The bloodstained head and staring eye
Of my old enemy. Go now to the settle,
Enjoy the merry feast, war-honoured one,
We shall great treasure share when morning's come.'

1785   Gladly the Geat approached the throne
As commanded the wise old king.
Then was after as before,
Valiant men along the floor
Renewed fair conversation. Night's dark helm
Over the gathering drew

1790   Warriors rose,
The aged, hoary Scyld retired,
The valiant Geat, so well renowned,
To rest inclined; a hall-thane soon
1795   Led forth the battle-weary one,
And all attentions proper showed
Which seamen in those days should need.
Rest to him, the valiant one,
1800   The vaulted hall towered gold-adorned,
Within slept the guest till the raven black
With joyful heart announced the dawn,

63

Then coming light shook off the night
And dark made haste away.

Then hurriedly the chieftain's men
Prepared to travel to their land,
1805   Eager to go, high spirited
As they drew near the ship.
He that bore hard Hrunting
Sent for Ecglaf's son,
Ordered him to take his sword,
The treasured iron.
Gave him thanks thus for the loan:
1810   Quoth that good he counted yon,
A war-skilled battle sword,
Reproached the blade not by a word,
That was a swordsman proud.

And when the war-like heroes
Were ready to be gone,
Went the hero of the Danes
1815   The atheling to the throne
Where the other war-chief was –
Greeting Hrothgar, Beowulf son of Ecgtheow spoke:

'Now we sailors, come from far,
Wish to say that we desire
1820   Hygelac to seek. Most kindly here
We were received,
Generously us thou hast endowed.
If on earth a whit I may
Of thine affection strive for more,
Leader of men, than yet I did
1825   In work of war, I'll be ready soon.
If I find out, gone over flood,
That neighbours threaten thee about,
As thee the enemy whiles did,
I will bring a thousand thanes
1830   Strong to thy aid.

'I wot in Hygelac, Lord of Geats,
Though he is young in ruling folk,
That he supports my words and deeds,
That I help thee and to thy aid
1835 Spears and men do bear at need.
* If yon Hrethric, royal prince,
Arrange to visit the house of Geat,
He will there find many a friend.
Distant lands are best explored
By him who is himself empowered.'

1840 Hrothgar said to him in answer:
'These words the all-wise Lord did send
Into thy heart, nor heard I greater sense
In such a young man spoken.
Thou art strong in might and great in mind,
1845 Wise councillor. I confidently hope
If it should happen that war's horrid claw,
The spear or sickness or the sword take off
Thy great ruler, Hrethel's son

'And thou yet hast thy life,
1850 That Sea-Geats can have none better
To chosen king, nor guardian stronger
Than if thy kinsman's realm thou'lt hold.
Long have I liked thy spirit well, dear Beowulf,
1855 Thou has accomplished that the folk
Of Geatish land and Gardane's realm
Peace shall share, and from ill deeds
Of war shall rest, which they before endured.
While I the wide land rule, be treasure shared,
* Across the gannets' realm the ship shall bring
1860 Over waters many another greeting good,
Gifts and tokens of friendship.
The folk I know with friend or foe
1865 Fast united stand, all steadfast as of old.'

Then Halfdane's son, the warriors' lord
Presented him yet treasures twelve,
Told him with the nation's love
Amidst these gifts to travel safe
And soon return.
1870   Then they kissed in firm embrace,
The noble king, the best of thanes,
Tears he shed, the grey old chief,
Honour and wisdom both were his belief,
1875   The other – that he from thence must see –
Advocate rather of audacity.
So much he loved this man that he
Could not forbear to weep,
But his heartstrings fast did yearn
Secretly for daring men
1880   With blood aflame.

From him thence Beowulf, laden with gold
Treasure-triumphant the grassland trod.
The ship awaited her master
Where at anchor she rode.
Then on the way were Hrothgar's gifts
1885   Counted repeatedly. That was a king
Faultless in everything, till age took from him
The joy of power, as it often does from many.

Came then to sea the noble troop,
1890   Ring-mail wearing, locked mail shirts,
The coast-guard, seeing the earl's returning,
Not as before, with insults, did greet
The guest from the cliff, but riding towards him
Quoth welcome the Geat, bright-armoured warrior
1895   To the ship faring.

There on the sand was the broad-beamed ship,
The ring-prowed with war-gear laden,
With horses and treasure – towered the mast
Over the presents that Hrothgar had given.

1900   He gave the guardian of the ship
A gold-bound sword, antique and rich,
That at the mead-bench afterwards
He was the more esteemed.

Then went aboard,
Deep water stirred,
Left the land of Danes afar.
1905   Sea-robes by the mast assumed –
The rope-fast sail – shuddered the spar.
Before the wind unhindered
Sped forth the ocean rover,
Foamy prowed sea voyager
Upon the main. Lept her stem
1910   Across the wave that they might see
The well-known ness, the Geatish cliff,
Then upward pressed, wind-driven,
And in land stood.

Quickly ashore the harbour watch prepared,
1915   He that had gazed long tides before
Ready for those dear friends afar,
Made fast the broad ship to the sand
With twisted warps, lest breakers' force
Might wreck the spendid bark.
Commanded then, the royal riches bore
Wrought and plated gold, he had not far
To look for treasure-giving.
Hygelac Hretheling himself was home
There with his court near the sea-wall,
1925   Splendid was built the famous king's high hall.

Hygd, quite young, intelligent, well-bred,
Though few the winters she had lived,
Haereth's child, beneath the citadel,
Though not she so miserly,
1930   Nor in gifts to Geats too niggardly,
Proud ways made the nation's queen most dread.

67

Of close attendants, none that dared
Brave the risk - except the prince –
1935   That her eyes gazed upon one day
But counted on a noose hand-tied
Assigned for him. Soon after then
*   Was grasped the sword decreed that it –
Patterened blade a-shearing – must
1940   Make execution known.
Such behaviour is not queenly,
That a woman be too ready,
Though she be a peerless wife,
In fancied insult to take life
For a man's presumption.
How Heming's kinsman ended that
1945   Other ale-drinkers told:
That she made no more distress
Maliciously, when first she was
Brought gold-endowed to the young prince,
The royal warrior; when Offa's hall
1950   Across the yellow flood she sought
(Bid by her sire the voyage to make)
Then well enthroned, in good repute,
She lived her life, held high in love
By a warrior prince of all mankind
1955   The best, I learnt, by seas between
Of mighty race; for Offa was
In peace and war widely respected,
A spear-keen man; wisdom ruled his land.
1960 *   Thence Eomor woke; to warriors' aid –
Hemming's kinsman; Garmund's grandson –
A crafty underling.

Then he departed, trod the wide firth,
Brave with his comrades over the sand;
1965   The world candle shone, the sun hasting south,
Their venture accomplished, went eagerly forth
Where the warrior's leader, Ongentheow's slayer,
Inside the fortress, the youthful war-king

1970   The heroes discovered at paying of rings.
        Hygelac soon was told of Beowulf's feat:
        That there came alive in fine array
        The troop to the fort, whole from the fray.
1975   All speedily made room as their lord bade
        The warriors returning enter court.

        They who survived adventure then sat down together,
        Brother with his brother, whereupon their leader
1980   With ceremonious earnest words greeted his overlord.
*   In mead cups Haereth's daughter, moving round the room,
        Loving then the people, gave the heathens wine.
        Breaking curiosity, Hygelac began
1985   To question his companion in that lofty room
        About the Sea-Geats' expedition:

        'How went the sea-voyage, Beowulf, my friend,
        When you of a sudden on combat resolved
        Distant to venture over salt water
1990   Warring to Heorot? But didst thou a whit better
        The widely known woes of famous prince Hrothgar?
        My heart seethed with sorrow, anxious my mind,
        Having no faith in the venture, dear friend,
        Long did I beg thee that thou not a whit
1995   The evil one tackle, let Southdane complete
        His own war with Grendel. Thank God I must say
        That here safe and sound do I see thee.'

        Said Beowulf, son of Ecgtheow:
2000   That is no secret, my lord Hygelac,
        The mortal clash of many warriors
        Upon a battle-ground, such mine with Grendel was
        Where many a crime he did perform
2005   Against illustrious Scyld, unceasing harm,
        I avenged all that, Grendel's tribe need not
        Boast on earth of that uproar at dawn,
        The longest lived of the hated race
        Seized by death. I came at first

2010   To that ring-hall, Hrothgar to greet.
Soon me this noble Halfdane's son
When he knew my inner thought,
Assigned with his own sons to the throne.

'Soldiers were friendly, I saw not far and wide
2015   Under heaven's vault a merrier room,
At times the splendid queen progressed the court,
A bringer of peace in nations, encourager of youth.
Oft she gave the warriors circlets wrought,
Before to the high seat going.
2020*   Whiles Hrothgar's bonny daughter bore
To earls the ale-jug round the floor,
Then heard I Freawar's name in court,
Where she gave warriors the studded cup.
Young, gold-endowed is she –
2025   Promised to the happy son of Froda,
So has friend Scyld agreed, the country's lord,
And counts on that alliance to settle strife –
To buy off the vendetta with this wife.
Often happens where a leader falls
2030   The death spear flies in but a little while,
Though the bride be beautiful.

'Great this affront to the prince of Heathobards
When he and the lady go to court,
The Danish princess followed by her train
2035   On whom the ancient heirlooms shine
That Heathobards have treasured for as long
As they have wielded arms,
Till in war their comrades laid
2040   The ring-mailed coats down with their lives.

An old spearman who remembers all men
Killed by spear (his heart is bitter)
Starts to stir resentment in young men
2045   Through secret thoughts, knowing their hearts,
Awakens strife with these words spoken:

'"Canst thou, my friend, recognise yon sword
Thy father took to battle under helm,
The last adventure of the treasured iron?
2050 Danes slew him there, ruled the battlefield
Where, after a hero's death, lay Withergield,
What Scylding of those now ordered here –
Unknown whose son – treasure-triumphant goes
2055 In court, wearing murder's boast and the heirloom
That thou shouldst rightly own."

'Thus he urges and each occasion his sour words remind
Until comes time that the lady's thane
For father's deed of ancient blame
2060 Blood-stained from sword gash dies;
Thence the other escapes alive –
Knowing the country well – on both sides then
Broken is the oath the earls have sworn.
2065 When harrassed Ingeld's emnity wells up
And for his wife his love cools down,
I reckon not those Heathobards will favour
Peace-treaties fast, alliance true, with Danes.'

2070 'I shall speak of Grendel forth again
That thou, bounteous ruler, knowest all
Of someone since become a wrestling champion!
When heaven's lantern the horizon graced,
Came the twilight horror fierce, the wrathful ghost
2075 Drew near us in the hall we guarded safe;
There Hondscio was stricken in the fight,
Mortal attack on the fated one, he foremost lay,
The girded warrior, thane of noble kin –
Him Grendel savaged with his jaws,
2080 The good man's body all devoured.

'Not while he again was empty-handed
Would the bloody slayer, murder-minded,
Go from the golden hall.
But my strength's measure he did try,

71

Hand to hand grasped readily.
2085 Wide and weird a glove was hung,
With cunning bonds was fastened on,
This all ingeniously adorned
With devil's craft and dragon's skin.
To me, guiltless, there within
2090 Frightful deed he would have done –
Of many, one. So he might not
In anger then upright I stood.
Too long to recount how I repaid
Every wicked crime against that land,
2095 Where I, my lord, thy people's worth established.
He got away – a short while life remained,
But in Heorot he left behind
His right hand; and thence he fled,
2100 Plunged in the mere in agony.

'For that success Lord Scyld gave
Many a treasure, much gold plate,
As my reward, when morning came
And we to feasting had sat down.
2105 There was story and song,
The aged Scyld, with learning filled,
Of old days did relate,
Whiles with sweet harp – the joyous wood –
Great deeds did salute;
Whiles tales recited sooth and sore,
2110 Whiles tidings right he told, and rare,
Whiles again, whom age did bind, the hoary warrior
Spoke to youth of mighty wars, hearts welled within
As by-gone years he did recall.

2115 'So we took pleasure all day long
Till another night upon men had come.
Then revenge was hastily prepared,
Grendel's mother sorrowfully journeyed
For the son death took through Weder's hate.
2120 The monstrous dam avenged her child,

A son of noble kindred killed,
There Aeschere was, wise councillor
Of many years, deprived of life;
Nor him they might when morning came
2125 The Danish clan, cremate with brand,
Nor on the pyre lay their dear one down;
That body she had carried off
In fiendish grasp beneath the stream.
2130 That was Hrothgar's deepest grief
Of all that long befell the chief.
Then in mood most desperate
This prince thy servant did entreat
That I should dive into the lake –
High rank adventuring glorious deeds!
He promised me reward.

2135 When I this torrent found –
Grimly perilous (it is well known)
There a while we grappled hand to hand;
Blood swelled the flood within that cell
And I cut off the head of Grendel's dam
2140 With giant sword. Barely thence with life escaped,
I was not done for yet. But me
The earls' Protector gave in turn
Many a treasure, Halfdane's son,
As by custom lived the king.
2145 By no means those rewards I'd lost –
Generous wages – but he gave me more,
Halfdane's son, on my own account.
'These I will bring thee, warrior king,
Gladly bestowing – all kindness yet
2150 On thee depends, little have I
Of closest kin, excepting, Hygelac, thee!'

He ordered then the boar's head emblem bring
The corselet grey, the war-steep helm,
The ornamental sword. This story told:
2155 'This armour Hrothgar gave to me,

Wise chief, some words commanded he:
That his esteem I first convey to thee.
Quoth that king Heorogar had it
A while long, the Scylding Lord,
2160   Nor ere this would give it to his son,
Brave Heareweard, the coat of mail,
Though he was true to him. Use all well.'

I heard that those four splendid horses,
2165   Matched dapple-yellow, filed in.
His rewards on him bestowing,
Riches and steeds, as men shall do –
Not wickedly for others weave
With hidden craft a net of death
For the hand that gives. A valiant man
2170   Was Hygelac, truly loyal his kinsman,
And each the other's pleasure shared.
The necklace I heard he gave to Hygd,
The wonder-gem that Wealtheow gave,
Royal princess, three horses too,
2175   Supple and saddle-bright;
She was thenceforth from receiving of treasure
Completely spoilt.

Thus did the son of Ecgtheow
Of men in war best known,
Uphold brave deeds with honour,
Slew not, when drunk, his thanes,
2180   Nor ever was of savage heart,
But, strongest among men, held fast
The precious gift God gave.
Was long despised, as Geatish men
Ranked him not high, not much honour
2185   At the mead-bench warrior chieftains
Would have done him; rather believed
That he was slack – a prince effete,
Good luck paid back the man for every slight.

2190	Then joyfully the earls' protector,
	The warrior bold in war,
	Sent for Hrethel's heirloom girt with gold;
	Not in all the Geatish land
	Ranked a more richly treasured sword
	That on Beowulf's breast he laid,
2195	And seven thousand holdings gave
	Him to rule (they both were heirs
	To wealth, dominion, land alike –
	The greater share to Hygelac).
2200	Came afterwards in later days
	The battle in which Hygelac fell
	And the slaughterous battle-sword
	Thrust beneath King Heardred's shield,
2205*	When Heatho Scilfing, warlike, hard,
	Pressing him in victory, sought
	Hereric's descendant. The wide realm then
	Passed to Beowulf's hand, he ruled
	Fifty wintertides all told, a prudent king:
2210	He was then old, the guardian of his land.
	Until, dark nights, a dragon's reign began –
	He that on high the piled hoard did guard,
	Steep mound of stone. A path beneath it lay
	Unknown to men. There entering in
2215	Some warrior stole a jewelled cup
	Of heathens' hoard, a wondrous handiwork,
	Richly adorned. He then that loss perceived,
	Though he asleep had been deceived
	By craft of thief. That people found,
2220	Men of nearby folk, that he was enraged.
	Not by force the hoard he broached
	By his own will, who so offended,
	But in great need this certain one
	Of warrior tribe, fleeing from punishment
2225	Needed shelter and hid therein – a guilty man.
	Soon the trespasser perceived
	That near him stood a dreadful thing –

75

Whether misshapen by the will of God
Or whether by man's wickedness was shaped.
2230   The warrior fled when him great terror seized,
The jewelled cup he took, many such there were,
Ancient treasures in that earthen house;
As they in olden days – certain men,
Noble heirs of great inheritance,
2235*   Taking thought, had hidden there the treasure rare.
Death took them all in bygone time
And one alone there yet
A veteran of his people, he
Longest there, became the guard,
Sorrowing for companions, awaiting a like fate,
2240   That he a little space of time
Age-long inheritance must own.
The plenished mound beside the water's edge
Lingered on the plain, new beside ness,
With cunning entrance safe. There within
2245   The treasurer carried earls' regalia,
The hoard-rich share of plated gold,
Few words he quoth:

'Now hold thou, Earth, now warriors may not,
The wealth of earls. What once on thee
Of power it got, violence destroyed –
2250   Mortal combat fierce cut down my people, every one.
None who gave these up – saw higher joys –
Wields the sword nor cleans the jewelled cup,
The flagon rare. Sup the brave elsewhere.
2255   Hard helm shall rust, glistening gold peel off,
When dies the polisher, then must
The burnished battle-mask, yea,
And each mailed corselet that war endured,
When biting iron broke upon the shield,
2260   Decay with warriors. Nor may armour ringed
Wide with heroes fare, by soldier's side,
No snatch of song the joyful harp may sing,
No good hawk wing beyond the hall,

2265   Nor swift steed beat the borough round.
           Many a man the flames of war despatched.'

           So sorrowing alone he mourned,
           The latest, last of all;
           Wretched passed his day and night
           Until death overwhelmed his heart.
2270   Then the old twilight raider found
           Open stood the treasure-hoard.
           War's naked dragon flies by night,
2275   Fire-surrounded, greatly dread by countrymen,
           Ancient barrows he shall seek, where heathen gold
           He guards through winters old
           Nor profits him a whit by that.

           So this genocide three hundred winters
           Held on earth some treasure-house
2280   Artful, withal, until one man
           Enraged his mood – to beg forgiveness of his lord
           Bore to the prince the plated cup.
           Then violate was the hoard, its treasure robbed.
2285   Granted, the wretch's plea, his prince
           Gazed the first time on the work of ancient men.

           When the serpent woke, war was renewed;
           Sprung from the stone, the black-heart found
           The raider's track – escaping he had trod
2290   With stealthy craft near to the dragon's head.
           (So the undoomed may easily survive
           Woe and exile, shielded by God's will).
           Would find the man who, while he slept,
           Did so offend; in hot and wrathful mind
2295   He circled oft about the mound;
           Not any man appeared in that waste land.
           But war's destructive work he did enjoy:
           Whiles turning to the cave, the treasure seeking,
2300   He soon found out that someone stole the gold,
           The noble cup; impatient then did wait

Till evening came.

When the barrow guard was angry,
Then many would in flame pay dearly
2305   For that rich cup. The viper longed
For day's departing, nor within walls
Would he lie waiting, but with flame-bursts
Urged the fire. This first assault brought terror
For the people of the land
2310   As swift upon their chief it brought
Violent end.

When the thing began to fire
Bright the houses burned,
Men stood fearful in the glare,
Not any living creature there
2315   The deadly flier would leave;
This serpent's war was widely seen,
The frightful onslaught near and far,
How the Geatish nation's foe
Terrorised and cowed; then sped the hoard
2320   The secret room ere daylight came;
Seized the land with flame and brand,
Trusted barrow, rampart, wall –
These hopes him failed.

When Beowulf was disaster told:
2325   Swift the truth, that his own home
The royal hall, the Geatish throne
Burned down – sad the heart of that good man;
His deepest grief this wise belief
2330   That he the Lord of Ancient Law –
Almighty God – did bitterly offend.
Dark thoughts unwonted welled his breast within.

From out the coastal fastness
Had the fire-dragon destroyed
2335   The stronghold of the nation pulverised.

Thus the war-king, Weders' Lord
His vengeance planned:
He ordered then a shield worked
All of iron, a wrought defence,
The warrior chief well knew
2340   Forests could not aid him,
Lime wood against flame.

The noble prince with ending day
Life's end awaited in this world,
And the serpent too, though long
The treasure-hoard he held.
2345   Then disdained the warrior chief
That he should seek the foe with troops,
With powerful force; not he to dread
The enemy, nor he this serpent's war a whit
Hardship he had faced before,
Many a narrow scrape survived,
2350   In violent clash of battle, till
With victory the swordsman blessed
Hrothgar's hall, and came to grips
In war with Grendel's hated kind.

2355   Not the least was that hand-fight
Where men slew Hygelac, Geatish king,
When he made war against the prince
Of Friesland nation; Hrethel's son
From gashes died, by sword beat down.
Thereafter Beowulf, returning,
2360   By his skill the water's span survived,
*   Had in his arm the strength of thirty
Men in mail when he did put to sea.
Nor had the Hetwar cause to boast
That they afoot bore shield against him,
2365   Few from that affray came home returning.
When Ecgtheow's son the river's width had swum,
To his land returned the last defender,
2370*   There treasury and realm Hygd offered him,

Crown and throne, her son mistrusting, that he could
Against invasion hold the throne with Hygelac dead.
No wretch by that could ever prove
At any council of the prince
2375   That he was Heardred's lord until
The kingdom would elect. However,
He upheld him in the nation,
Advisor, in honour and esteem
Until he was of age to rule the Geats.

2380* The exiled sons of Ohthere [Eanmund and Eadgils]
Sought Heardred over waters, Hygelac's son.
They had defied the Scilfing Lord,
Greatest sea-king of those from Sweden's realm
Dealing treasure out – a famous prince.
That was the end of Hygelac's son,
2385   For that he paid with mortal wound,
Sword swung, and he in turn,
Ongentheow's son went home when Heardred fell;
The throne he left to Beowulf
2390   To rule the Geats, that king was good.

This prince's fall in later days
The son of Ecgtheow requited,
Exiled Eadgils he befriended,
Over water's wide supported
Followers of Ohtere's son
2395   With arms and troops; avenged him when
Cold disaster overcame the king.
So every venture had survived – hardest battles –
Ecgtheow's son did valour's work until the day
2400   That with a dragon he should fray.
Then went some twelve in angry grief
To find the dragon; the Geatish chief
Had heard then who aroused this feud,
The flames of war; the precious cup
2405   Came through a spying hand into his own.
That was the thirteenth member of the band

80

That caused the outbreak of the war;
Thence in remorse would he lead on
2410   Knowing the plain, reluctantly went
To the earthen mound that only he did know,
The cave beneath the ground near water's flow
By tumbled stream. This was full within
Of gems and wire, the awful guard
Ready for war had held the treasury
2415   An age beneath the ground.
No sweet objective that for any man to gain.

Then on the hillside sat the warrior king
While his companions wished their lord farewell;
Sad at heart he was, restless and death-ready,
2420   The infinite drew near to greet the prince,
Seeking the captive spirit,
Sundering body from life; not long
Would flesh contain the valiant soul.
2425   Said Beowulf, Ecgtheow's son:

'Many a skirmish I endured when young
In time of war, that I remember, all.
Seven years I was when King Hrethel
His nation's friend, most generous lord,
2430   Took me from my sire to rule and train,
Clothed and fed me, mindful of our kin.
Nor, while he lived, aught less he loved me,
A child at court, than his own sons,
Herebeald and Heathcyn and my Hygelac.

2435   'Was for the eldest spread outrageously
By brother's deed, a bed of death,
When Heathcyn did with arching bow
Strike him with arrow in mist's murk,
2440   One brother by another's bloody shaft
Was by his kinsman shot.
That was violence with no redress,
A fearful wrong to break the heart,

81

Should either thus, though he a prince,
Unavenged from life depart.

*   'Sorrowful it is that an old man lives

2445   To see his child ride upon the gallows young;
Then he sings a mournful song
That feasting ravens hangs his son
And he may not do anything
To aid him – old and reverend.

2450   Sorrow is remembered every morning,
His son's departing;
Another heir in court
He cares not to await
Whose first one's debt to death
Has by death been met.

2455   Sad he looks upon his child's home,
The empty wine-hall where the wind doth rest
Of noise bereft. The horsemen sleep,
Warriors in the grave
Where no sweet harp of yore
In the courtyard plays.

2460   Goes then to the inner room,
Mourns his sorrows one by one,
Land and homestead seem too large to him.

'So for Hearebeald the Weder king
Broke his heart in grief;

2465   No whit could he avenge that violent death
Nor hate the warrior that did the crime –
Though unloved he was.
Then he, with sorrow overcome,
Gave up companionship of men,

2470   Chose God's light, his children left,
As good men do, lands and townships
With his life, laid down.

'Then across the waters rode
Accusations of offence

82

Mutually by Swedes and Geats,
Stirred trouble up when Hrethel died
2475 Till to his son
Ongentheow's became war-minded, battle-ready,
Would not keep peace across the sea
But near Hroesnaburh repeatedly
Brought terror and hostility.

2480 'That my kinsmen fierce avenged,
As it was learned, though one paid dear,
Heathcyn was, the Geatish king,
At that bettle slain.
Then I heard that in the morning
One friend avenged another's slaying,
2485 With iron blade, where Eafer sought
The aged Scilfing, Ongentheow.
War-helm shattered, battle-pale,
Many scores the hand recalled,
Nor stayed the swinging blade.

2490 'Him I repaid as chance allowed
In war for treasures that he gave,
With gleaming sword. He gave me land,
Ancestral home, did Hrethel's son;
No need for him to seek among
2495 Gifthum, Gardanes, nor in Sweden's realm
For worse warriors,
Always on foot I went before –
In the van alone;
And always shall do battle so
As long as lasts this sword that now,
2500 Then and often has availed.

'When I before the army came to grips
With Daeghrefn, Huga champion,
Not he then to the Friesian king
Wealth to deck his breast might bring,
2505 But fell the standard-bearer in the fight –

83

A noble prince; sword was not the slayer,
But war-grip stifled, broke his frame,
Now shall sword's edge, hand and stout blade
Fight for the hoard!'

2510   Beowulf vowed, the venture nearing:

'In youth have I many battles braved.
Now, guardian of the folk in age,
I will fight, the victory bright
2515   If this earth-dweller seeks me out!'

Then greeted he his men each one
Who bore the helmet this last time,
His dear companions.

'Never would I weapons use
Sword on the serpent, if I knew
How else I might fulfill my vow
2520   Against the monster, as I did
With Grendel once.
But I expect hot flames of war,
Fumes therein and poisoned air,
So shield and shirt of mail I bear.
Nor the barrow's guard I'll flee
2525   A foot exact, but there shall be
The outcome at the wall decreed
By Fate, the judge of every man.
My mood so firm that I disdain
To boast against yon battle-dragon.
Wait ye armed upon the hill,
2530   Men, prepared for who best will
From combat's grip return between us two.
Not your fight this, but mine alone,
He who with monsters tries his strength
2535   Must be an earl.
With honour I shall gain the gold, or battle claim
In fatal combat fierce, your king!'

Then rose the famous warrior with his shield,
His mail wearing hard beneath the helm,
2540 Trusting the strength of a single man alone –
No coward venture that, beneath the cloven stone.
Then he, who many wars had known,
The battle-clash of men on foot,
2545 Saw by the wall an arch of stone
Whereout a stream broke from the mound;
There were surging waves of hot wild-fire,
Not near the hoard unburned he might –
For the dragon – any while remain.

2550 Rage in his breast at the hindrance,
The Weder-Geat Lord shouted aloud,
Angrily stormed. Came the war-cry echoing
Underneath the ancient stone.
Fury was roused. The guard recognized
2555 The voice of a man. No time for parley,
At once came a monstrous puff
Of hot war-gas from out the stone,
The cavern dinned.
Under the barrow the Geatish Lord
2560 Against the enemy swung his shield,
Then was the ring-bowed heart prepared
Battle to seek. The valiant king
Brandished his sword, the heirloom old,
Not dull, its blade. Each combatant
2565 Was of the other feared.
Staunch with shield steep stood Valour's friend,
Swiftly, tightly, coiled the serpent then,
He waited, armed,
Went the scorcher, arching, gliding
2570 Swift towards destiny.
Less time the shield well guarded life and limb
Than sought the valiant prince for his intent.
That day the first time that he must prevail
As one decreed no victory by Fate.

2575	Hand upraised, the Geatish Lord
	Swung so terribly the ancient sword
	That failed its blade, bright on bone
	Beat less ready than its noble king,
	Hard-pressed, had need.

2580	Then was the barrow's guard,
	At that great blow, in furious mood
	Wild-fire flung – wide sprung the battle-flame
	No victory the Lord of Geat did claim,
2585	The war-sword failed at naked need
	(It should not so – the iron most good)
	That was no easy task
	That this great Ecgtheow's son
2590	Should wish elsewhere his place on earth
	As all men shall – allotted fleeting days.

	Not long was then
	That frightfully they met again,
	The treasure-guard took heart, drew breath,
	Advanced anew; agonized in rings of flame
2595	Him who once a people ruled.
	No troop of comrades stood him close,
	The noble challenger,
	But hid them in the woods, their lives to shield.
	Remorse seized the heart of one in shame,
2600	They that think well never may
	From kinsfolk turn a whit away.

	Wiglaf was named Weohstan's son,
	Valiant squire of Scilfing clan,
	Aelfhere's kinsman saw his chieftain
2605	Under war-helm suffer burning.
	Then honours earlier given him remembered he,
	The rich steading of Waegmunding,
	Every domain his father owned;
2610	Then to seize the yellow linden shield
	His hand could not forbear,

*   He drew the ancient sword that, with his life,
        Eanmund, Ohter's son, had left.

        At that battle the exiled warrior
        Weohstan slew with edge of sword,
2615   And from his kinsman took the burnished helm,
        The armour ringed, the ancient blade –
        O'Nela gave that to him, his kinsman's mail,
        The gear of war; spoke not of the feud
        Though he his brother's son had killed.
2620   He kept the treasure many a year,
        Bill and birnie, until his son
        Might be an earl even as his father;
*   Then amid the Geats he gave
        Uncounted arms to everyone
2625   When he from life went, aged, on the way.
        This was the young warrior's first affray
        That he should share war's onrush with his lord
        Nor did melt his heart, nor ancient sword
        Weaken at war – as the serpent found
2630   When they had met together. Wiglaf spoke –
        Many true words to his comrades said –
        His heart was sad:

        'I recall those times when mead we drank
2635   When we promised to our Lord in hall
        Who gave us these arms,
        That if upon him came such need as this
        Of helmets and stout swords, we would repay.
        Then from the army he chose us to make this journey,
2640   His own desires reminding us of glory,
        And me these treasures gave when us he counted worthy
        To bear the helm. Though our Lord
        Has thought to do this noble work alone –
2645   For he most mightily performs of men
        In valiant deeds – now day has come
        That our leader has great need
        Of brave companions; let us go to

Help our chief as long as heat inflames
2650 This fire-terror. God knows in me
I'd liefer that my body with my lord's
The flames embrace; nor think I fit
That we bear shields returning home
2655 Unless we first bring down the foe,
Defend the life of Weder's Prince;
I know for sure that by no ancient score
Does he deserve alone of Geatish men
To suffer death, to fall in war.
Swords and helms we shall,
2660 Arms and mail, share alike.'

Then went he through the reek of war
To aid his lord the helmet wore;
Few words quoth he:
'All count least, beloved Beowulf!
As thou in youth didst say of yore
2665 That thou wouldst never let thine honour sleep
Whilst thou didst live, now shall high deeds
Princely resolution, all effort life defend.
I follow thee!'

Upon these words the furious dragon came
2670 The dreadful foe another onrush made
On hated men, fire blazed –
Flame burnt the shield round;
No cover the young spearman's armour gave,
2675 But brave he dodged beneath his kinsman's shield
When fire destroyed his own.
Then mindful of glory yet, the famous king
Struck with battle-sword a blow so strong
That forced into the head it stood –
2680* Naegling broke.
Beowulf's sword failed in the fight.
Grey and old, no iron might him in combat aid,
His hand so strong that every sword
2685 His swing did overtax I heard,

When he took the wound-hard blade to war
No whit the better, he.

Then a third time was the enemy
The fierce fire-dragon, minded for the fray,
2690   Rushed on the brave when he gave room,
Close seized his throat with piercing bane,
The fearful stream, the life-blood, ran.

Then I make known throughout the folk-king's need
2695   The skill and courage of a noble earl
(As by inheritance he was)
Thus he heeded not the head but burnt his hand,
Courageous man, where he helped his comrade;
In nether parts he struck the evil thing -
2700   Knight in armour – that that sword sank in –
Shining and plated – that that fire began
Thenceforth to wane. Then the king, himself again,
Used his wits, drew out his seaxe,
Bitter and sharp, that he wore in his shirt,
Slashed the worm in the centre through.
2705   The Wederer chieftain felled the foe
Valour avenged life, and both of them
Had brought him down – kinsmen, noblemen,
So a knight should be – servant at need!

That was the last occasion for the prince
2710   His deeds on earth brought victory.
When the wound the dragon earlier gave
Began to burn and swell, he found
2715   That soon within his breast the poison spread.
Then the prince, going past the wall,
Sat thoughtfully in the recess,
Saw in the work of giants how
Arch of stone with column fast
Held the great earth-fort within.
2720   Then with his hands the loyal thane
With water washed the bloody stain

From his dear chieftain, famous prince,
Wearied in war, and his helmet loosed.
Beowulf spoke above his mortal wound,
2725 Well he knew at end for him
The day-time of earth's joys;
When measured days were gone
And death, unmeasured, near:

2730 'Now would I give my armour to my son
Were such given me to follow on,
An heir from my body sprung.
Fifty years this nation I have ruled,
There was of neighbouring princes none
2735 That durst greet me in war fear-threatening;
I have stayed the destined time on earth,
Held my own, sought not to oppress,
Not many swore me oaths unlawfully.
2740 In all this, weak in death, I may rejoice
That God need know in me no murderer
Of kinsmen, when life my body leaves.

'Now go thou quickly, search the hoard,
2745 Wiglaf, love, beneath the mossy stone.
Now the worm lies dead of his sore wound
Treasure-bereft! Be now in haste
That I may see the ancient hoard,
The shining gems, the artful gold,
That I by this pleasure may
2750 From richness of my treasure, yield
Life and kingship which I long have held'

Swift, I heard, then Weohstan's son
At his stricken lord's command,
2755 The ring-net wore, the mailed shirt
Underneath the barrow's roof.
Then, blessed with victory, he saw,
Passing the entrance unafraid,
Rich gold a-glitter on the ground,

Wonders on walls and this worm's den.
2760 The old night-flier. Beakers standing,
Cups of bygone men that polish lacked,
Reft of ornament. There was many a helm
Rusted and old, many a bracelet
In battle secured. Easy treasure,
2765 Gold in the ground, overthrows the mind
Of everyone – deny it who will!

Such he saw: a banner all of gold
Hung high above the hoard,
Marvellous handiwork, skillfully stitched.
2770 Stood the light that he could see the floor,
The intruder looked around:
There was not any sign of Worm
But – Blade had demolished him.
Then upon that mound I heard
One man ransacked the giants' hoard,
2775 Loaded his breast with dishes
And vessels of his choice,
The bannar too, bright beacon, carried off.
The earlier broken sword
(The blade was iron, an ancient lord's,
He who kept the treasure guard
2780 Long whiles, kept before the hoard
Hot surging flame at mid-night, till
He tasted death).

In haste to leave, the eager messenger
Pressed forward, anxious, with his loot,
2785 Wondering if he would meet his lord alive
Where he had left him stricken mortally.
Then, with the treasure, found the Weder Lord
2790 Fatally bleeding, close to life's end;
Water he dashed on him again
Till speech broke from confining breast,
Age looked upon youth's gold:

91

'For all the riches here I gaze upon
2795   Say thanks to God eternal, wondrous King,
That this for my nation I have won
Before I die.
2800   Now dearly have I laid my old life down,
Sold at my people's need,
I may not be here long.
Command the warriors build a grave
Bright after blaze at water's edge,
So to my nation shall rememberence
2805   Tower high on Hronesness
*   That Brentings may call it Beowulf's barrow
When ships drive far over darkening seas.'

His golden collar the royal prince
2810   Gave his young warrior thane,
His jewels, mail and burnished helm,
Use them well, he bade:
*   'Thou art the last of our Waegmundings race,
2815   Fate has drawn all my kinsmen to their doom,
Earls in valour. I shall after them.'
Those were the veteran's last words,
His heart's last thoughts, before he chose
The pyre's consuming flame.
From his body went the soul
2820   Seeking judgement's truth.
That went hard with the untried youth,
Seeing the life most dear on earth
At end, was sadly borne.
The slayer also lay, the dread earth-dragon,
2825   Bereft of life, destroyed in war,
No longer might the serpent bowed
Rule the treasure-hoard, but him
Iron blade destroyed – hard, war-scarred
2830   By hammers left – that wide-flier collapsed,
Wound-still on earth beside the treasure-house;
Never after to appear
Jewel-proudly speed the mid-night air,

92

| | But he had fallen to the ground |
| 2835 | Before the work of valiant hands. |

	Truly, in that land there were
	Few men who had the power, I hear,
	Though they in all things daring were,
	That they with poisoned fumes contend,
2840	Or in the ring-hall stir a hand
	If they a watchful guardian found
	In occupation of a mound.
	Beowulf had paid with death
	For that share of treasure rich,
2845	Life's loan had reached an end for both.

	Then by no means was it long
	That those cowards left the wood
	Ten troth-tardy liars together,
	That had not dared before a javelin speed
	At their steadfast chieftain's need
2850	But they in shame their shields bore
	Where the old one lay, their arms.

	They gazed on Wiglaf, he wearied sat,
	Foot-warrior by his leader's shoulder,
	Wet him with water, no whit him recalled,
2855	Nor might he on earth, though well he desired
	Hold life within the gallant lord.
	Not thus God's doom averted,
	Each man's deeds the Almighty ruled
	As yet now He doth.

2860	Then easily was angry answer born
	At those young men who earlier honour lost;
	Wiglaf spoke, the son of Weohstan,
	The sorrowful swordsman gazed in disgust:

| | 'That tale he may recite who likes truth spoken |
| 2865 | That this great chief who gave you yonder arms – |

The gear of combat in which here ye stand –
That at the ale-bench he often gave
To hall-thanes – corselets and helms,
Finest anywhere, the prince his men,
2870   Far or near which he could find –
That he threw away these arms complete
When grievously in war he was beset!
By no means need that Chieftain boast
Of his companions in the fray
Even though God granted victory
2875   That he alone with his own sword prevailed.
Little cover could I give in the fight,
And began as though beyond me measured
2880   A comrade's helping. The fight was failing
When my sword struck the enemy – was weaker ever –
The fire already less determined surged.
Too few defenders thronged the leader close
When his hour came.'

*   'Now shall endowments and sword-gifts,
2885   All joys of home, love of your kindred, cease.
Must each man's land-right of this tribe become
Void, when kings afar do learn your shame.
2890   Ignoble deed! Better is death
For any earl than life disgraced.'

He ordered then the war's outcome proclaim
Up above cliff's edge, where the earl troop
All the morning sorrowfully sat
2895   Shield bearers in hopes of both
Ending day and the beloved's return.
Less silent was the messenger who rode the Ness,
But all he told over, truthfully:

2900   'Now is the Giver of Weder nation's gifts,
The Lord of Geat, upon his death-bed fast.
That bed of death the serpent's deed sustains;
Beside him lies the mortal foe, seaxe-bane sick,

94

2905	No sword could on that monster work a wound.
	Wiglaf over Beowulf sits, Weohstan's son,
	One earl over another – dead.
	That weary heart the head-watch holds
2910	For loved – and loathed.
	Now is the nation's prospect war,
	When to Frank and Frieslander
	The King's fall is widely known.
	Hard with the Hugas was this quarrel shaped
	When Hygelac came upon the Fries
2915	Sailing his ships. Then the Hetwar attacked
	Him in war – rushed eagerly with greater force,
	That this armed warrior should give way,
	Fall among the infantry.
	No booty gave his veterans the Prince,
2920	Friendship's been denied us ever since
	By the Merovingians.

	'Nor hope I from the Swedish king
	A whit of troth or peace,
	But widely known it was that Ongentheow
2925	Took the life of Heathcyn Hretheling
	When in arrogance against Ravenswood
	First sought the Geatish lord Guth Scilfingers.
	Soon he, the wise one, Ohter's father,
	Old and terrible, the onslaught turned:
2930	Killed the sea-rover, released the bride,
	The aged dowager of gold deprived –
	O'Nel's mother and Ohter's.
	And followed them with mortal emnity
	Till they escaped with difficulty
2935	In Ravens Holt, without their lord.
	The wounded-weary remnant then
	The great array besieged,
	All night long to the wretched band
	Repeated threats of woe:
	Said in the morning they would come
	With swords to get them, sport with some

2940   Upon the gallows tree.
    Just at first light help arrived,
    When, in desperate mood, they heard
    Hygelac's horn and trumpet calling.
    Then the good king came with men
2945   In their footsteps following.

    This bloody swathe of Geat and Sweon,
    The armies' clash was widely seen,
    How war awakened midst these folk.
    Then went the king with his companions,
2950   Old and wise, the stronghold sought,
    Withdrew afar, Earl Ongentheow,
    Had heard in war proud Hygelac's skill,
    Mistrusted resistance, that he might beat
2955   The Seamen's Chief, the fort protect,
    Children and wives. Then turned at bay –
    Old, behind his earthen walls.

    Then the hunt was on for the Sweon clan;
    Forth Hygelac's standard the stronghold then
2960   Overwhelmed, when Geats rushed the ramparts.
    There Ongentheow was brought to a stand,
    The grey-haired king at point of sword,
    Eafer's only decree – that the king should submit,
2965   *But him in a rage Wolf Wonreding hit.
    Swept his blade, that from the swing
    Beneath his hair the life-blood sprang,
    The old Scilfing was not afraid,
    But swift with a worse exchange repaid
2970   Him for attack upon the king.
    Nor could this hasty Wonred's son
    Give the old man a counter hack,
    But he on his head had split the helm
    That, stained with blood, he must fall back,
2975   Sink to the ground. Not yet dead he,
    But recovered himself, though the wound was deep.
    The stalwart thane of Hygelac

*   (Eafer) when his brother fell,
           Broke through the shields with giant old sword
2980   Crashing on helm. Then the King went down,
           His people's warden, mortally stricken.

           Then were many that his kinsmen bound
           Quickly raised up, when he was removed
           That they might control the battle field.

2985   Then one warrior despoiled another –
           Took from Ongentheow the armour,
           Hard-hilted sword and helm alike,
           The veteran's gear to Hygelac bore.
           The treasure he took, and promised him fair
2990   Reward and lands, and thus fulfilled it:
           'Hrethel's son, the Lord of Geats,
           Gave the warriors, Eafer and Wulf,
           When they came home amidst great wealth,
           Paid in reward to each of them
2995   A hundred thousand marks of land
           And golden chains.
           No man on earth had cause to blame
           Him for those gifts their prowess won,
           And to Eafer he gave then
           His only daughter to grace his home –
           In favour to wed.

           'That is the strife and the quarrel,
3000   The warriors' feud have I thus:
           The people from Sweden will seek us
           When dead they hear is our prince.
           The one that held against foemen
           Ever the hoard and the realm,
3005   After the fall of the chieftain
           Who gave to the Scyldings solace
           And valour surpassed.

           'Haste to me is best

That we look to the chieftain there,
And bring him that gave us riches
3010 On the road to the funeral pyre.
Not merely one that shall melt with the brave,
But of treasure there is a store –
Gold uncounted, grimly won, and now at the last
Rings bought with his life the flame shall consume,
The fire enfold.
3015 No earl wear the treasure for souvenir,
On no maiden's throat the jewels shine,
But in sorrowful mood, bereft of gold,
Often, not once, shall tread strange land.

3020* 'Now has the warrior laid down laughter,
Gaming and song. Whence many cold mornings
Shall fingers grip spear raised in the hands
Of a warrior that wakes to no harp's sound.
3025 But the raven wan broods over the fallen,
Many a speech to the eagle he makes:
How in haste at the feast
He did race with the wolf
To despoil the slain.'

What the swordsman thus said was sad telling,
Not many his words fate belied,
3030 Warriors arose, their tears welling
Went under Earnaness sorrowing
Wonders to see. Then found on the sand
Lifeless lay he who had given them rings
3035 In seasons gone by.
Then was ended the day
Gone the valiant away
When the war-king of Geat died a wondrous death.

There first they saw the strange creation
3040 Where lay across the ground the dreaded worm;
The grim battle-stained fire-dragon
Was smirched with flame; fifty foot long

a-lying measured that once the night air ruled,
3045 Thence downward departing near to the den
Death-fast was then – had ended the watch
At the cavern in earth.
By him stood flagons and vessels,
Lay discs and ornate swords
Rusted throughout, as if they in the ground
3050 A thousand winters had there endured.
There were the age-skilled heirlooms,
Gold of the men of yore,
Bound by a curse that no man might touch
3055 Unless God Himself, victory's judge –
He is man's help – granted that he
Should open the hoard – even that man
As He thought deserved.

Then it was seen that the venture throve not
For them who within, unrighteous, had hid
3060 The treasure hoard under the wall.
First the guard slew one among few
Then fiercely the debt was repaid.

Unknown where the valorous earl
Fares at the end of life's destined spell,
3065 When no longer a man with his friends
In the wine-hall may dwell.

So with Beowulf when he sought
The barrow's guard in war, himself knew not
Through what his death should come about;
3070 So till doomsday kings renowned
Solemnly proscribed it:
They there pronounced
That that man be guilt-condemned,
To the heathen groves confined,
Fast within the bonds of hell
Wracked with grief, who robbed the place:
For him no ownership's esteem

3075   Of the gold which once he gazed upon.

Wiglaf spoke, Weohstan's son:
'Oft shall many earls endure
Punishment for one's desire,
As to us has come about.
We could not tell the dear-loved Prince
3080   The kingdom's Lord, not to approach
The warden of gold, but let him lie
Where long he was – stay in his earth
Till the end of the world,
Held in God's destiny.
Uncovered the hoard is, grimly won,
3085   Too harsh was fate that drew him on.

'I was therein and saw all that –
The ready store, when chance allowed,
Not sweetly was the passage gained
Under the earthen wall within.
3090   Much I seized with hasty hand,
A heavy burden rich bore out
Here to my king; then was yet
His speech of sense and wit,
Much he spoke in age and pain,
3095   And to greet you did ordain,
Bade that ye build for your Prince's deeds
A pyre, a barrow, high and great
As was he of men – of warriors noblest,
World-famed widest,
3100   As long as the rich capital he ruled.
Away now in haste, the riches to see,
And seek the strange gems piled under the wall;
Guide you I shall that ye near enough look
At treasures and plated gold.
3105   Make his bier ready when we come out,
And then bring our friend, beloved of men
Where long in God's keeping he shall remain.'

3110　Then ordered Weohstan's valiant son
　　　Many a man, householders, bring
　　　Firewood afar for that good king:

3115　'Now in the dark a towering flame
　　　Shall devour a chieftain famed
　　　Who oft withstood the iron rain
　　　Shaken over shield walls, the arrow storm,
　　　Held taut, the shaft in feather-garb
　　　Followed the barb.'

3120　Next did this wise Weohstan's son
　　　Call from the company seven men
　　　The highest of royal thanes;
　　　Some eight of them together went
　　　Warriors beneath the roof of dread
3125　One bore in hand a lamp who went in front.
　　　By them was no apportioning
　　　Who ransacked the hoard,
　　　When unguarded any share
　　　Remaining in the cell they saw
　　　Lie wasting, little any cared
3130　That they carried out in haste
　　　The treasures rare.
　　　Then shoved the dragon over the cliff,
　　　Let the wave carry off the guard to the deep;
　　　Then on the wagon was laid the wound gold
3135　All uncounted, borne with the bold,
　　　The warrior grey, to Hronesness.
　　　The Geatish people built for him
　　　Unsparingly on earth a pyre,
3140　Hung with helm, bright birnie, shield
　　　As he had willed;
　　　Laid in the centre the famous Prince,
　　　Mourned for the hero, the dear-loved chief,
　　　Then began on the barrow the great death-fire,
　　　Raised for a warrior,
　　　Wood smoke arose

3145   Dark above the blaze,
Drowned the noise of mourning
In the roar of burning,
Wind's riot dropped till the body broke hot
In fire's heart.

Sad in mind lamented they their leader's death.
3150   Such woeful tales told the Geatish prophetess,
With unbound hair sang of grievous care,
Much her remaining days bewailed
That dreaded she, with murder filled,
Men defeated, humbled and enslaved;
3155   The smoke did heaven enfold.
Then built the folk of Weder Geat
A howe on the hoe, so high and broad
Seen afar by sailing men
And completed in days ten,
3160   Beacon of the battle-bold.
Ash from the brands with a wall surrounded,
Most worthily made it as men could devise,
Laid in the barrow riches and treasure,
All such adornments before in the hoard
3165   As men heeding temptation removed.
Let earth hold earls' treasure
In cavern of gold,
Where now it stays yet –
Ages as useless as ever was it.

Then round the grave rode warriors twelve,
3170   Nobly descended, the children of earls,
In sorrowful speeches to mourn for the king,
The tale in words framing, of bravery telling
Concerning his kingship and valiant works;
The veterans deeming in words, as was fit,
3175   That a man for love of his dear leader's spirit
When from life's bondage it rises, shall praise it.
So mourned the Geatish folk their lord
3180   Men of his household said that he was

Of earthly kings the most benign,
Of men the mildest and most kind,
To his folk most merciful,
Most eager for renown.

NOTES

4   Shield Sheafing was the mythological ancestor of the Danish royal dynasty, the Shieldings, or Scyldings.

17   This Beowulf Scylding is the first non-mythological member of the Scylding dynasty. The poem's hero is named after him in order to remind the audience of Ecgtheow's feat in killing the enemy of the Scyldings and re-instating them upon the Danish throne. This is rather similar to Roman custom when, for instance, the Emperor Claudius called his son Britannicus to remind people of his own exploit in conquering Britain.

12-51   The story of the funeral in a blazing ship was made well-known in the early 20th century by Baroness Orzski in her famous novel Beau Geste. She made it a Viking funeral, but here it seems to predate the Vikings by some four hundred years.

59-63   Besides the names mentioned here, there was also a King Helgi (10), another brother of the Scyldings; it may be that the scribe got confused over Helgi and Helga, for the rhythm breaks down and about two syllables are missing. The queen's marrying Heatho Scilfing seems clear and fits the Saga of Hervor and Heathrek. Their son in that case would be Ongentheow - the Angantyr of the Saga.

82-85   The hall was burnt down by Hrothgar's kinsman Hrothwulf in a war of succession with Hrothgar's sons after his death. This is referred to at lines 1019 and, with dramatic irony, in Wealtheow's speech at 1228.

86   The tale of Grendel and his mother, lone survivors of a primitive race - strong, but not particularly intelligent - must be one of the oldest stories there is. The Greek legend of primitive Titons - where the Titon Prometheus is said to have learnt all he knew from his mother, an earth goddess, seems related to it. The Sherpas of Nepal have a similar tale about the Yeti. This was recorded by Tom Stobart, camera man with the 1953 expedition to Mount Everest. He went back to the region the following year to gather material for a book about the Yeti. He was told how there were once many Yeti, who raided the Sherpas' fields. They laid an ambush and so wiped out the entire race except for one pregnant female who escaped; she had a son, and any existing Yeti are said to be descended from this lone female and her son.

305   A small divergence from the usual translation which involves the cheek-guards of a helmet now in the British Museum. I think the passage refers to the carved boar's head on the prow of the ship. No matter.

454   Hrethel belongs to the mid-fifth century, he probably died in the 470's. He was father of Heathcyn and Hygelac, and was probably the son of Swerting of line 1203. He may have been named after Hraedla, a fourth century hero of the wars between Goths and Huns.

459   Hrothgar remembers how Ecgtheow, Beowulf's father, slew Heatholaf/Heathrek and so restored the Scylding dynasty to the throne in place of Heathrek, who had usurped it. To commemorate his exploit, Ecgtheow calls his son Beowulf after the first non-mythological Scylding king. Ecgtheow was most probably a real person, in fact the Jute Octha, son of Hengest, of the Anglo-Saxon Chronicle. Octoviri were praetors in Roman times (25) -several of the Beowulf names sound like Greek or Roman official titles, the administration may still have been in place at the more junior levels. Hrothgar tells how when he came to the throne he made peace with the Wylfings and Heathobards who swore him oaths of allegiance. Both these names seem to

indicate Swedes.

612   Queen Wealtheow, Hrothgar's wife, was probably English, or East Anglian. See The Origin of Beowulf by Professor Sam Newtown (32).

865   I am told that in modern Norway the native breed of pony is dapple-yellow, so Heorot may be thought of as situated in Southern Norway. As in the modern New Forest, most of the ponies are mares.

875   Beowulf was a Jute on his father's side and a Geat or Goth on his mother's, so the poet's tales will be chosen to compliment his ancestors and tell the warriors in hall who their visitor is. The famous story of Sigemund (Siegfried) was in honour of the Geatish/Gothic side.

898   Worms, serpents and dragons may have been mechanical flame-throwers using naptha to produce 'Greek fire'. The technology did exist in the poet's time. This dragon melted.

898-915   To make sense of the Sigemund story, you have to take every alternate 'he' or 'his' as referring to Sigemund, and every second 'he' or 'his' as referring to Heremod until you get to lines 913 and 914 at the end (almost) which refer to Beowulf or possibly Ecgtheow.

1016   Hrothgar and Hrothwulf were kinsmen. Hrothwulf was known in Scandinavia as Rolfe and is known from Gregory of Tours to have once visited the Emperor Theodoric the Goth, ruler of the western Roman Empire. Rolfe is said to have settled the Danes in the Danish islands, where the town of Roskild is named after him (Chambers) this would account for his absence from our poem. It was he who burnt down Heorot.

1044   'The Ingwine's ruler'. This could perhaps be taken to mean that Hrothgar's empire extended over the territories of the tribe the Roman Tacitus called Ingevones. Geographically that seems perfectly possible.

1068   Hrothgar's poet now tells of the adventures of Hengest and his Jutes in compliment to Beowulf, who is Jutish on his father's side. Modern ideas of honour would not let us admire Hengest's sneaky behaviour in getting Finn slain at second hand by giving him a sword which is bound to bring the fury of Ordlaf and Guthlaf upon him. They, returning from a voyage, see the sword of their brother Hunlaf and immediately assume that Finn must have killed their brother. By this time Hengest has left Finn's court and so does not even witness the slaying of Finn by Ordlaf and Guthlaf which he had caused to happen.

1198-1210   This refers to events in 374 AD. Eormenric was head of a loose confederacy of Gothic peoples stretching from the Black Sea to the Baltic. He was descended from the Amali, a great family among the Goths. He was defeated by the Huns and committed suicide in 376, aged 100, so they said.

Hama, also a Goth, left the army of Eormenric taking with him some immensely significant Gothic regalia - the Brosings' necklace. For Hama to have been a Brosing, as his possession of the jewel suggests, makes him likely to have been 'Hama-Brosingas' that is Saint Ambrosius of Milan, chosen by the Great Council of the Goths to be its Bishop in 374 although he was not yet even baptised. The poet may be being pius in saying that he 'chose greater council' since Ambrosius got baptised and so chose God.

The poet's mention of Swerting at line 1203 suggests that Hygelac inherited the necklace, but we are not told

107

how Swerting got it - perhaps he took part in a barbarian raid on Italy, he or some ancestor of his. He was the son of King Soemil who first separated Deira from Bernicia (says Nennius) (2).

1203 Swerting is the Sguerthing of Nennius (2), son of Soemil who first separated Deira from Bernicia'.

1205-1213 This passage is confirmed by Gregory of Tours in his History of the Franks. He calls Hygelac 'Chochilaicus' so the name was not immediately recognised, but when it was, scholars were able to work out that Hygelac was killed in 521 AD.

1557 It is arguable that all the Beowulf's swords are known in legends. If so, this one might be the sword Mistletoe of the Sagas. For a modern example of an ancient bronze sword hanging in a cave beside a river, see Wild Swans by Jung Chang, page 536 of the paper back edition published by Flamingo 1993.

1836-1840 Prince Aldfrith - the author of the Beowulf (23) would have been familiar with the Roman author Protagorus, who wrote '...a man has to be careful when he visits powerful cities as a foreigner...' (Quoted in OU Course A293, Supplementary Texts p.47).

1859 By happy coincidence, Gannets breed in Britain only on the Yorkshire (Deira) coast.

1935-1940 This sword sounds like Tyrfing, the sword of the Scylfings. It was made by the Dwalin for Arngrim the Berserk, the ancestor of Ongentheow (8). It was last heard of in the hands of Heathrek who murdered his brother with it. (Saga of Hervor and Heithrek). The legend of the sword was that, once it was unsheathed, it must kill somebody (8). It would now be in possession of the Geats, either because Ecgtheow slew Heithrek and would have brought the sword back to give to Hrethel Geat, who was Ecgtheow's overlord. Or, if Ongentheow son of Heithrek, had managed to rescue it before he escaped, then it would have fallen into the hands of Eafer when he killed Ongentheow, and Eafer gave all Ongentheow's armour and war-gear to his overlord, who was Hygelac. So either way, the sword Tyrfing would have been among the Geatish regalia. A warrior was under an obligation to give any loot from his exploits to his overlord. The overlord would then reward the warrior as he saw fit.

The convention that Queens were often paramount meant that the sword would probably be deemed to belong to Queen Hygd, Hygelac's wife. She married a second time after Hygelac's death, with Offa/Wuffa of East Anglia. If she took the ancient relic with her it no doubt ended up in a barrow (it had at one time been buried with Angantyr the son of Arngrim, but was dug up by Hervor, his daughter). So the sword is yet another candidate for identification with the Sutton Hoo sword.

The custom at naval courts martial of placing an unsheathed sword on the table pointing towards a man who had been found guilty would be an interesting subject of research.

1943-1949   The fact that Queen Hygd has now become 'peerless' or 'matchless' as some translators have it, suggests that some older Queen has died and Hygd is now the paramount Queen among the Picts, Scots and perhaps even British. She has no social equal.

1950   Because of her rank, her father has no difficulty in arranging a second marriage for her to the young king Offa/Wuffa of East Anglia. The yellow flood may be the Wash - perhaps she traversed the same route where King John was to lose the crown jewels 700 years later.

1965   It appears that from her marriage to Offa was descended Eomer. His attempt to assassinate King Edwin of Deira was foiled by the devotion of two thanes. (Anglo-Saxon Chronicle). Since this happened in 625 AD, Eomer would have been a descendant of Offa and Hygd, not their son. Many people would disagree with this interpretation, and it is not of primary importance here, especially as the text is damaged or at least dubious.

1967   It was Eafer who slew Ongentheow, but the overlord of a warrior not only received all the loot, but was also credited with killing the enemy. (Wrenn) (1).

1982   Hygd has not yet perpetrated her wicked deed in getting a man executed as we saw at 1.1943. She gives wine to the 'heathens' according to the English custom; 'but Hygd was probably a Christian, and tramping about the room handing out the booze may have been a cultural shock. Hygd may have regarded herself as a descendant of Cleopatra through the Egyptian Queen Scota from whom Haereth's daughter would have been descended according to legend. (Annals of Ulster).

2020-2068 Evidently when Heathrek led the Danes into Denmark and drove out the Jutes by defeating Withergield, quite a lot of Swedes came along as well, since Heathrek was, though in exile, a Swede. He had always had a body-guard of people from his native land; it seems likely that the Heathobards are also Swedish followers of Heathrek. Hrothgar tries to appease them and unite the country of Denmark by marrying his daughter to the Swedish king, so that any Swedes in his own kingdom will be loyal to the Scylding dynasty. We know from the Sagas that this did not work, and here Beowulf foretells that it will not.

2205   This Heatho Scilfing would be Weohstan, who we know was a Scilfing because his son Wiglaf is said to be a

Scilfing at line 2603, even though he is the last of the Waegmundings (descended from Waegdaeg, presumably). After Weohstan slew Heardred as told here, and Eanmund as told at 2614, the Geats changed sides and accepted Weohstan as their ruler.

2237-2269   The poet seems to have drawn inspiration from the story of the bard Merlin (not the magician) who is said to have been born in the 470's (31). '...After he had been present in many battles, on one disastrous day between the years 560 and 574, in a field of horrible slaughter on the Solway Firth, he lost his reason, broke his sword, and forsook human society, finding peace and consolation only in his minstrelsy. He was at last found dead on the bank of a river. (Morley. English Writers. 1. 218. Quoted in The Times Century Cyclopedia of Names. 1900).
For the broken sword see line 2778.

2361   A word is lost in the manuscript, but Hrothgar at line 379 says that Beowulf was supposed to have the strength of thirty men.

2363   The Hetwar were a Frankish tribe; the Attuarii on the lower Rhine (1).

2370-2379   Beowulf becomes regent for Heardred. It seems likely that this is true to the extent that someone probably became regent for the boy king. His father, Hygelac, was killed in 521 (19), so the regency probably lasted about seven years at least.

2380-2400   Evidently the throne of Sweden had fallen vacant and Eadgils got there first and took it, despite the fact that his father had prior claim. His father, Ohthere/Arthur/Ottar set out with an army to frustrate his son, but his force was ambushed while taking a short cut through Lymfiord in Northern Denmark (9),

Ynglinga Saga says there was a frightful battle and Ottar was killed (9). His body was given no proper burial, but left out to feed the crows. The poet does not mention this in so many words, but at line 3020 a passage begins which suggests that he is reminding us of it. It comes in the middle of Beowulf's grand funeral where everything was done lavishly and properly; the sudden reminder of the unburied warrior draws our thoughts back to Ottar/Ohthere. The later poem 'The Twa Corbies' (Palgrave's Golden Treasury) seems to be a memory of this event.

2445 Eormenric, ruler of the Goths, who has already been mentioned, is said to have hanged his eldest son (31). Heathcyn of course was not hanged but lived to be king. The seeming irrelevance of this passage about a son hanged may be a reminder of the death of Eanmund even though he was killed by a sword. Irrelevance seems to be a device the poet uses to turn our thoughts to other events beside those he is speaking of.

2612 Weohstan was a Scilfing, (2603) so in slaying Eanmund he is killing his own kinsman. He may be the Wehha of East Anglian pedigrees (20). Eanmund was Ohter's eldest son; it is not clear why he rebelled against his father. I hope by now the reader understands that Ohter and Arthur are the same individual so we have some idea where Eanmund was killed and buried. After the defeat of the Geats he seems to have retreated, perhaps into Lincolnshire and down the Fosse Way, until driven off it by the proximity of the enemy.

'There is another wonder in the country called Ergyng (Archenfield near Hay-on-Wye). There is a tomb there by a spring, called Llygad Amr; the same of the man who is buried in the tomb was Amr. He was a son of the warrior Arthur and he killed him there and buried him.' Nennius 73.

As with Hygelac being called 'Ongentheow's slayer' when the deed was done by Eafer, so Ohter would not have slain Eanmund with his own hands, but Ohter was the overlord of Weohstan, so the deed is attributed to him. Similarly Onela the half-brother of Ohter has Eanmund's death attributed to him at line 2630, though line 2614 plainly says that Weohstan killed him.

2624   The defeated Geats now come under the sway of the Scilfings. In fact, the Geatish royal dynasty has died out with the death of Heardred, probably about 530 AD.

Weohstan/Wehha was perhaps connected with those Swedes whose country was in East Anglia. Remains of a Swedish culture have been found by archaeologists with boat burials similar to those of Uppsala (34).

2680   The procession for the enthronement of Bishop Jenkins to be Bishop of Durham was shown on television. The regalia included a broken sword carried on a suitable cushion. The commentator remarked that the legend of this sword was that it was broken in a fight with a dragon. Perhaps it is Naegling.

2806   It seems likely that the Brentings were the Brigantes who had lived in Deira and Bernicia since Roman times. They would still be there as farmers and fishermen no doubt. It is possible that the Bryd of line 2130, Ongentheow's one-time wife and mother of Onela and Ohthere, had been their queen. Her capital may have been Stanwix, where once Queen Cartemandua is thought to have reigned. The Bryd would simply have found herself surrounded and overwhelmed by the Geats, with whom she probably made a deal. Whether she relished being rescued from the comfortable inactivity of her old age by the ferocious Ongentheow, we do not know. He needed to reestablish the marriage to get the loyalty of the Brigantes and so undermine the Geats.

2814   The Waegmundings may have been the Jutes, who were descended from Waegdaeg, according to pedigrees in Anglo-Saxon Chronicle and elsewhere.

2884   We are probably approaching the last quarter of the sixth century; exile and slavery are looming for what is left of the Geats. More in this vein at line 3017 and 3150.

2965   The name Wonreding means 'woeful council' since Wulf's behaviour at this council does seem to have been ill-advised, it is likely that his father's name was not actually Wonrede; but that Wulf acquired the name as the story was repeated. It is interesting that his helmet was split and the resulting head-wound made him fall to the ground bleeding profusely so that Eafer and probably everyone else, thought he was dead. In Culwch and Olwen (14) the head of the senior Boar is said to have been split in two and the Britons considered they had killed him. The Beowulf poet says he recovered though the wound was deep.

        The whole passage from lines 2925 to 3005 is probably a description of the battle of Catterick of, roughly, 500 AD, plus or minus five years. The casualties on the British side are lamented in the poem Y Gododdin (13). It lasted a week.

2978   As mentioned in the Introduction, Eafer fits well as King Ida of Northumbria - he only became king for the last twelve years of his life. The Anglo-Saxon Chronicle gives 547-559 as his dates. His slaying of Ongentheow described here could have been when he was a young warrior engaged in his first important enterprise, say, about twenty. His later adventures, in the 530's perhaps, are probably those described in the Mabinogion's (14) tale of Culwch and Olwen where he is called Twrch, the Boar. One of his fortresses may have been the town of

York - Eaferwiccaester was its Anglo-Saxon name. Later his capital was Bamburh, which he fortified when he became king.

3020-3028 This passage is an irrelevancy because Beowulf was certainly not left out to feed the eagle or the wolf but was buried with all fitting ceremony. But we know who was left unburied - King Ohter, the Ottar of Ynglinga Saga, and as for Arthur: 'Annoeth beith bedd y Arthur' no-one knew where the grave of Arthur was. (The Black Book or Carmarthen - The Verses of the Graves translated by W.F. Skene, edited by Derek Bryce) (16). It is possible that when Onela led an expedition to avenge the death of Ohter he may have collected the remains from Lymfiord and given them proper burial in Sweden before Onela and his army themselves perished. I say this because Chambers mentions a barrow in Sweden called Ottar's barrow.

GLOSSARY OF PROPER NAMES

Abel (108) The Biblical Abel.

Aelfhere (2604) Wiglaf's kinsman, a Scilfing.

Aeschere (1324) Elder brother of Yrmenlaf.

Beanstan (524) Father of Breca.

Beowulf Scylding (17) The first non-mythological Scylding king of the Danes.

Beowulf first mentioned at line 344. Son of Ecgtheow, he is the hero of the poem, A Jute on his father's side, Geat on his mother's. Fictional, but may be based on someone.

Breca (521) Son of Beanstan; they were Brondings.

Brondings (521) A tribe. Possibly the Brandanes of the Isle of Bute in the Hebrides.

Bryd (2903) Pictish or British Queen of Brigantes. Sometime wife of Ongentheow, mother of Ohter and O'Nel.

Cain (107) The Biblical Cain.

Daeghrefn (2501) a Huga warrior. Perhaps a warlock as Beowulf was.

Danes. Inhabitants of, mainly, Norway, Denmark and the Danish islands.

Eadgils (2392) Rebellious son of Ohter. He afterwards became king of Sweden.

Eafer (2486, 2977, 2993) 'The Boar' Twrch of Mabinogion's Tale of Culhwch and Olwen. Afterwards King Ida of Northu mbria. Son-in-law of Hygelac and Hygd, great-great-grandfather of the poet Aldfrith if the Ida/Ea for identification can be accepted.

Eanmund (2611) Eldest son of Ohter and grandson of Ongentheow. He is the Amr, son of Arthur of later legends. Killed by Weohstan. Nennius 73 tells of his grave.

Ecglaf (499, 590) father of Unferth, a Gardane.

Ecgtheow (262, 373, 460, 470) Father of Beowulf. Probably the Jute Ochta, son of Hengest,

116

grandson of Withergyld, slayer of Heathrek/Heatholaf, the father of Ongentheow.

Ecgwela (1710) A dane.

Eomer (1960) Grandson of Wuffa/Offa the East Angle, and Queen Hygd. See Anglo-Saxon Chronicle 625 AD for his attempt on the life of Edwin of Deira at the behest of the king of Wessex.

Eormenric (1200) Died 376 AD. Ruler of a loose confederation of Gothic tribes stretching from the Baltic to the Black Sea.

Finn (1068, 1081, 1096, 1146) King of the Frisians in the 5th century. Killed by Oslaf and Guthlaf who thought he had killed their brother Hunlaf.

Finland (580) May be Mull, land of the MacKinnons, or Lapland, if preferred.

Fitela (879) Nephew of Sigemund.

Folkwald (1089) Father of Finn.

Franks (2912) They were then part of the realm of Theodoric the Goth.

Freawar (2020) Hrothgar's daughter, whom he married to Ingeld.

Frisians and Frisland were Hygelac's nearest continental neighbours, whom he invaded. (2915, 2357).

Froda (2025) a king of Heathobards and father of Ingeld. Their dynasty was the Wilfings.

Gardanes (1, 601, 1856, 2495) Danes at Hrothgar's court.

Garmund (1960) father of Offa/Wuffa, elsewhere known as Wermund and Waermund.

Geats (443 and throughout the poem) The royal family of Deira during the second half of the fifth century and until about 530 AD. Descended from the same ancestors as Gaut, Algaut, and Gautrek the Mild of Sweden.

Gifthum (2494) The Gepidae, an East Germanic tribe.

Grendel (381) The monstrous foe of the first half of the poem. Based on a very old legend.

Guthlaf (1148) Slayer of Finn. He and his brother Hunlaf may be the Hunthiof and Gunthiof of the Saga of Frithiof. A Dane.

Haereth (1929, 1981) Father of Queen Hygd of Geats. Haereth appears to be Herth, or Mac Erc, High King of Northern Ireland.

Heathcyn (2435) King of Geats after Hrethel, he accidentally slew his brother Herebeald and so became king before Hygelac. Killed by Ongentheow's forces around 505AD.

Heathens (1983) pagans, like most of Hygelac's followers, but contrasted with Haerethas, the retinue of Queen Hygd, who may have been Christian.

Halga (61) Danish queen, wife of Heatho Scilfing, mother of Ongentheow, see Hervor and Heithrek's Saga.

Hama (1198) Saint Ambrosius of Milan. ('Ham-brosing').

Halfdane (57) A scylding King, Hrothgar's father.

Heardred (2369, 2373, 2385) Last Geatish king. He succeed-
ed his father while still a boy, but as a young man befriended Eanmund and Eadgils and so was killed by Weohstan.

Heathobards (2037, 2067, 2024). A tribe headed by Froda and then Ingeld, defeated by the Danes after the death of Heatholaf/Heathrek, they may therefore have been Swedes.

Heatholaf (459) appears to be the Heathrek of the Saga of Hervor and Heathrek and of the Saga of Heathrek Wolfskin and would therefore be father of Ongentheow. Not totally certain, but a good fit.

Heatho-Reams. Romerika of Norway, or Heth and Rhum of the Hebrides (Heth an ancient name for Tiree, says Skene).

Heatho Scilfingas (62) Heathrek, Ongentheow's father, husband of Halga. The Heatho Scilfing of the line 2205 cannot be the same as that at 62 as the two sets of events are some fifty years apart. 2205 could be Weohstan.

Helming (620) Wealtheow's family.

Hemming (1944, 1961) an Angle.

Hengest (1083, 1091, 1127) The historical Hengest.

Heorogar (61, 467, 2158, 2155) Elder brother of Danish king Hrothgar.

Heorot (67, 81, 720) Hrothgar's hall.

Heoroweard (2161, 2658) Son of Heorogar.

Herebeald (2434, 2462) Elder brother of Heathcyn, son of Hrethel Geat, slain by Heathcyn.

Heremod (901, 1709) Legendary bad Danish king of the fifth century or earlier.

Hereric (2206) Ancestor of Heardred, grandfather of Queen Hygd, the Irish King Erc.

Hetware (2363, 2916) Historical Frankish tribe of the lower Rhine, the Atruarii of Chattuarii)

Hildeburh (1071, 1114, 1157) Mother of Hnaef, wife of Finn, she was Danish.

Hnaef (1069, 1070, 1114) A Dane, son of Hildeburgh.

Hoc (1076) Father of Hildeburh, a Dane.

Hondscioh (2076) The Geat warrior slain by Grendel.

Hreosnaburh (2477) Roxburh or Corbridge or fictional.

Hrethel (373, 1923, 2462 etc) King of Geats, fifth century. Father of Herebeald, Heathcyn and Hygelac, son, possibly of Swerting.

Hrethric (1189, 1226, 1836) slain by Hrothwulf in Norse tradition, he was the son of Hrothgar.

Hrothgar (59, 465 etc) King of the Danes, he appears to have ruled over the Ingwines and received oaths of allegiance from the Wylfings, the royal family of the Heathobards.

Hrothmund (1189) Son of Hrothgar.

Hrothwulf (1014, 1163) He became king after Hrothgar having displaced Hrothgar's sons. A historical figure (Rolfe) he visited Theordoric the Goth.

Hrunting (1457, 1490, 1659, 1807) Unferth's sword.

Hugas. Frankish tribe (2501, 2914).

Hunlafing (1143) The sword of Hunlaf, brother of Oslaf and Guthlaf.

Hygd (1926, 2202, 2369) Queen of Geats, daughter of Haereth and so a Scot from Northern Ireland on her father's side. Mother of Heardred and of Eafor's bride. She may have been British on her mother's side. Her second husband was Wuffa/Offa of East Anglia.

Hygelac Geatish king.

Ingeld (2024) Son of Froda. They appear to have been Wylfings, the royal dynasty of the Heathobards. Supporters of Heatholaf, they were not reconciled to their defeat by the Danes even though they swore Hrothgar oaths of allegiance.

Ingwine (1044, 1310) The Ingevones of Tacitus. They owed allegiance to Hrothgar.

Merovingians (2921) The royal dynasty of the Franks.

Naegling (2680) Beowulf's sword.

Offa (1949, 1957) Wuffa of East Anglia, the second husband of Queen Hygd.

Ohtere/Ohthere (2928, 2611, 2380, 2394) son of Ongentheow, nominally king of Sweden, but his attempt to wrest it from his son Eadgils ended in disaster at Lymfiord (3). Born in Britain, he has come down to us as King Arthur, though that name is not thought to have existed during his lifetime. He was a real person, claiming (according to Arthurian legend) to rule Norway, Denmark and Lochlyn (Sweden) as well as leading all the armies of the British and Pictish kings.

Onela (2616, 2932) It is not really necessary to the case for a Geatish Deira to alter present views on Onela; he is thought to be son of Ongentheow and brother of Ohthere. But the poet does not say that Onela was son of Ongentheow, only that Onela and Ohthere had the same mother. He may the The O'Neal, a nephew of Haereth, born in Ulster and leader of a people from Galway who settled upon the north shore of the Solway Firth (Skene) they were called the Nellan. He went to Sweden to avenge the death of Ohthere, but perished there with his army in a winter campaign.

Ongentheow (2923, 2924, 2928, 2930, 2933, 2941, 2961, also 2387, 2924, 2951, 2986). A Swede presumably the son of Heathrek/Heatholaf, he is not listed among Swedish kings (27) but Heathrek, at the time of his death, ruled Norway and Denmark and was allied to the Heathobards, himself being a Swede. Ongentheow was therefore a Swede and a king by inheritance, since the Swedes had probaby owed allegiance to his father Heathrek. By his marriage to a Pictish or British princess or Queen, he was also royal enough in Britain to lead an alliance of British kings. So he was both a Swedish king (Perhaps not King of Sweden) and the legendary Uther of medieval tales.

Oslaf A fifth century Danish warrior on the side of Hengest against Finn.

Ravenswood, Ravensholt (2925, 2935) A wood in Deira.

Scyldings The Danish royal dynasty and their followers.

Scilfings Ongentheow, Ohthere and their relations. Heathrek in the Sagas is not usually called a Scilfing. It could be that the name came through Ongentheow's wife, since the royal family of Albion was called Silvan (35), which would Anglicise as as Shilfing.

Sigemund The Siegfried of Gothic legend, to the Geats a great hero.

Swedes Ongentheow's and Ohtere's people in the male line of descent.

Swerting (1203) Hygelac's grandfather, the Sguerthing of Nennius 61. King of 'Saxland' (Saxo Grammaticus) Northumbria was 'Saxonia' (Adamnan) and 'Seaxlaib' (Book of Leinster (23)).

Unferth (499, 587, 1167, 1455) A cowardly spokesman of Hrothgar's, who lent Beowulf his sword and it broke.

Waegmunding Beowulf's father's dynastic name; the Jutes derived their ancestry from Waegdaeg. Wiglaf was also a Waegmunding as well as being a Scilfing so he must have been half Jutish.

Waels (879) Father of Sigemund.

Waelsing (877) Son of Waels - the Volsung of that Saga, i.e. Sigemund.

Wealtheow (612, 664, 1162, 1215, 1188) Hrothgar's Queen. May have been English (32).

Wederers The Geats, from their proximity to the river Wear, Ptolomey's Vedra (5).

Weland (455) The famous Smith.

Wendels (348) The Vandels.

Weohstan (2602, 2611) Father of Wiglaf. A Scilfing, slayer of Eanmund and Headred, he then brought the Geats under Scilfing control. Possibly Wehha of the pedigrees(20).

Wiglaf (2603, 2604, 2661, 2809, 2813, 3076). A Scilfing and a Waegmunding, son of Weohstan.

Withergyld (2051) Seems to be Whitgils, the father of Hengest, but leader of the Jutes in Denmark who were defeated by Heathrek. Grandfather of Ecgtheow.

Wonred (2971) The surname of Wulf, it meant 'woeful council' and refers to his attack on Ongentheow.

Wonreding (2965) Wulf, as above.

Wulf (2964) Brother or half-brother of Eafor, he may also be the 'Ysgithyrwyn, Chief Boar' of Culhwch and Olwen. Both had their heads split open (14).

Wulfgar (348) A Wendel chief.

Wylfings (29) The royal dynasty of the Heathobards, followers of Heatholaf/Heathrek, but after his defeat, swore oaths of allegiance to Hrothgar.

Yrmenlaf (1324) A Dane whose brother Aeschere was eaten by Grendel's mother. (Fictional).

BIBLIOGRAPHY

1. Beowulf Ed. C.L.Wrenn. George Harrap. 1953.

2. Nennius Ed. & Trans. John Morris. Phillimore. 1980.

3. Chronicles of the Picts Ed. & Trans. J.F. Skene.
   H.M. Treasury. 1867. Includes Welsh and Irish additions to
   Nennius.

4. Annals of the Picts Ed. J.F. Skene
   Chronicles of the Scots H.M. Treasury c.1905
   Annals of Ulster

5. Origins of English History Lord Elton.
   (for Ptolemy's map) Bernard Quaritch 1802.

6. The Anglo-Saxon Chronicle Ed. & Trans. Garmondsway.
   Everyman (Dent).

7. The History of the Franks Gregory of Tours, Penguin Classics
   1974.

8. Stories and Ballads of the Far Past Trans. N. Kershaw.
   Cambridge
   (for Hervor and Heathrek's Saga)University Press. 1921.

9. The Heimskringla Trans. S. Long. Dent.
   (for Ynglinga Saga)

10. Three Northern Love Stories Trans. Eirikr Magnussen and (For
    the Saga of Frithiof) William Morris. Longmans. 1901.

11. The Saga of the Volsungs Trans. Margaret Schlauch. The
    American Scandinavian Foundation. W.W. Norton New York
    1930. Page 85 chapter xiv for Otr.

12. Anglo-Saxon Poetry Garmondsway. Everyman (Dent).

13. Y Gododdin Aneiran. Trans. A.O.H. Jarman. Gomer Press 1990.

14. The Mabinogion Trans. Gwyn Jones and Thomas Jones.
(For the tale of Culhwch and Olwen) Everyman Dent 1975.

15. The Concise Oxford Dictionary of English Place Names
Ekwall. Oxford University Press.

16. Arthur and the Britons in Wales and Scotland
(For the Verses of the Graves, verse 42) W.F. Skene, Ed. Derek
Bryce. Llanerch, Lampeter.

17. Roman Britain Peter Salway. OUP 1990.

18. Anglo-Saxon England Sir F. Stenton. Oxford Clarendon Press.

19. Introduction to Beowulf R.W. Chambers. Cambridge University
Press.

20. The Anglo-Saxons Ed. P. Clemoes. Bowes. (For the possible
Weohstan/Wehha suggestion by Nora Chadwick in the chapter
on The Monster and Beowulf).

21. King Arthur's Avalon Geoffrey Ashe. Collins 1957.

22. The Kingdom of Northumbria AD 350-1100 N.J. Higham. Alan
Sutton 1993.
Page 170 has a picture of an important comb.

23. Northanymbre Saga John Marsden. Kyle Cathie Ltd. 1992. (For
King Aldfrith, likely author of Beowulf).

24. Open University Course A 293. Supplementary texts, and course
book Rome, the Augustan Age Chisholm and Ferguson.

25. From the Gracchi to Nero H.H. Scullard. Routledge.

26. The Celtic Empire 1000 BC - 51 AD Peter Beresford Ellis. Constable. Page 162.

27. The Heroic Age of Scandinavia G. Turville-Petre. Hutchinson University Library.

28 The Saga of Heathrek Wolfskin, called The Saga of King Heathrek the Wise
Ed. Christopher Tolkien. Nelson. Icelandic Texts.

29. Y Geiriadur Mawr H. Meurig Evans, W.O. Thomas. Gomer Press.

30. OU Course A 205 Culture and Belief in Europe. Page 412 for Queen Clothild and cutting hair.

31. The Times Century Cyclopedia of Names. 1900.

32. The Origins of Beowulf Sam Newton. D.S. Brewer.

33. The Sherpa and The Snowman Charles Stonor. 1955. Hollis & Carter.

34. The Archaeology of East Anglia R. Rainbird Clarke. Thames and Hudson.

35. Celtic Scotland. A History of Ancient Albion W.F. Skene. Edmiston and Douglas. Edinburgh. 1876.

INDEX

Remembr
Sunday

by
Andrew K. Jones

Research Student at Spurgeon's College, London

GROVE BOOKS LIMITED
Bramcote   Nottingham   NG9 3 DS

CONTENTS

ACKNOWLEDGEMENTS

I would like to thank Colin Brown, Greg Forster and Charles Hutchins for their help and my wife Eleanor for much inspiration.

Andrew K. Jones

THE COVER PICTURE

is by Peter Ashton

First Impression April 1987

ISSN 0144–1728

ISBN 1 85174 051 1

INTRODUCTION

Remembrance Sunday can be the most difficult of all Sundays for the sensitive pastor. What we are doing or thought to be doing can be an emotive as well as an emotional issue. Problems of whether the day should be observed at all, and if so how, are exacerbated by the passing of the years, nuclear arms, and more recent campaigns, such as the Falklands.

In our congregations we may find people from many nations, including Germans and Japanese. We may find those who fought, those who refused to fight, as well as people too young to have experienced war at first hand. But there will also be those for whom Remembrance means renewed feelings of pride and guilt; of pain and grief. Our stance in this booklet is that of the pastor in the local church, rather than of commentator on Remembrance at National or Cenotaph level.

First, a brief introduction to Remembrance Sunday. Its roots take us back to the end of the First World War and the commemoration of Armistice Day. This is how *The Times* prepared its readers for that first anniversary in 1919:

> 'The king invites us to keep it with him in a manner worthy of the great deliverance vouchsafed to us and to mankind twelve months ago. In the sanctuary of our hearts he bids us commemorate that day; and commemorate those who died to achieve it. At 11 a.m. the hour when the Armistice came into force the whole peoples . . . will turn for two short minutes to these thoughts—to thanksgiving, to rejoicing, to pity, to a life-long pride and grief . . . remembrance of "the glorious dead" . . . we can conceive no service worthier.'[1]

Contradictory emotions and tensions evident in that article were drawn out even more sharply by the *Baptist Times* one week later:

> 'Trafalgar Square was gay with flags . . . the crowd was sombrely clad and very quiet.'

The writer observed the poignancy of the procession . . .

> 'not the pomp and pageantry of war but literally the maimed, the halt and the blind.'[2]

It was not until 1946, after World War Two, that Armistice Day was changed to Remembrance Sunday.

Many of the moral problems for both pastor and congregation associated with Remembrance Sunday reflect attitudes to the nature of war itself. Consequently, the first section indicates some of the principle attitudes to war. This is followed by a look at the history of attitudes to Remembrance from 1918 to date. The concept of duty found in these two sections is then offered as a moral basis for Remembrance. We then consider the people involved—the pastor and congregation, before examining the service itself. More detailed discussions are given to the prayers, the sermon and the eucharist in the Remembrance service.

We conclude that, seen as a duty, Remembrance Sunday ought to be observed in our local churches, though not necessarily as in the past. Our motive, the means of observance, and the probable outcome of our approach are deemed all-important considerations.

[1] *The Times,* (7 November 1919), p.13.
[2] *Baptist Times* (And Freeman), (14 November 1919), p 673.

1. CHRISTIAN ATTITUDES TO WAR

In our congregations on Remembrance Sunday we can envisage a continuum of attitudes to war ranging from pro-military to totally pacifist. Robin Gill, in *A Textbook of Christian Ethics,* lists four responses:

(1) Thoroughgoing Militarism—the willingness to fight anywhere, at any time, and for any cause.

(2) Selective Militarism—the willingness to fight when one's country or state declares that the cause is just.

(3) Selective Pacifism—the willingness to fight only when one is personally convinced that the cause is just.

(4) Thoroughgoing Pacifism—the unwillingness to fight anywhere, at any time, and for any cause.[1]

With the exception of thoroughgoing militarism, the ethic of the mercenary, it is reasonable to expect the other three attitudes to be present at a Remembrance Sunday service. Whether and how one feels Remembrance Sunday ought to be observed will be influenced by these attitudes to war. The pastor should be aware, even today, of the potential tension between those for whom war is anathema, and those who see the day as a celebration of God-given victories. Furthermore, there may also be tensions within individuals trying to come to terms with the apparent contradictory demands of the state and justice on the one hand, and a personal loving of one's neighbour in obedience to Christ on the other.

Gill's attitudes can be consolidated under two headings, Pacifism and Non-Pacifism. We will review pacifism first.

Pacifism

Two forms of the pacifist argument are offered by George Thomas, in *Christian Ethics and Moral Philosophy.* The first is the religious argument that war is 'contrary to God's will and inconsistent with faith in Christ.' The second, the ethical argument, is that war is 'morally wrong, contrary to man's conscience as well as God's revelation.'[2]

Pacifism in general is argued from biblical, historical, pragmatic, and emotive standpoints. Biblically there is offered the non-resistance, non-violent example of Jesus and his the Sermon on the Mount.

Historically Gill discerns what he describes as a fundamental dichotomy between the pre-Constantine and the post-Constantine churches. Gill contends that Christianity became other than pacifist only with Constantine.[3] In support of his view Gill cites Tertullian's contention that in disarming Peter, the Lord 'unbelted every soldier.'[4] He also quotes Origen's defence of Christian pacifism, that it did not undermine the state because of the incalculable contribution made by the 'army of piety—by

---

[1] Robin Gill, *A Textbook of Christian Ethics* (T. & T. Clark, 1985) p.296.

[2] George F. Thomas, *Christian Ethics and Moral Philosophy* (Scribner, New York, 1955).

[3] Gill, *A Textbook,* p.297

[4] *Ibid.,* p.298.

offering our prayer to God.'[1] It ought to be noted, however, that Gill's historical argument appears difficult to sustain in the light of Cadoux's magisterial work, *The Early Church and the World.*[2]

The pragmatic argument for pacifism is that wars seem to create as many problems as they are intended to solve. There is much emotive argument.

In the pacifist tradition have stood the sixteenth century Anabaptists, and stand today such churches as the Quakers and Mennonites, as well as many individuals in other churches.

The plight of the conscientious objector is evidence that pacifism includes a political element. Many Christian pacifists support peace movements which are explicitly political. In recent years renewed interest has been shown in the Peace Pledge Union, and their adopted alternative symbol, the white poppy.[3] An insight into some of their views will help pastors as they prepare for Remembrance Sunday.

In 1986 the Peace Pledge Union objected to the participation of politicians at the Cenotaph, because of 'the inconsistencies between mourning the dead of past wars while providing the fuel for current wars with the supply of arms overseas.'[4] Again, defending the use of the white poppy, they wrote 'we feel that the war disabled, both civilian and military, should not have to depend on sales of red poppies for adequate support but should receive full government help.'[5]

Whilst the Peace Pledge Union has always been political, there has been a discernible shift in its attitude to Remembrance Day. The founder, Dick Sheppard, concerned by the excesses of some early victory celebrations, urged the need 'to retain for Armistice Day the setting of solemn reverence and gratitude in which a people may retain its duty both to the living and dead.'[6]

These notions of gratitude and duty to the dead were given less prominence in subsequent Peace Pledge Union writings, much greater weight being given to the future. Vera Brittain wrote the following in 1961:

'A Remembrance Day widely marked by humility and penitence would be a challenge to the world to start again. The present threat of nuclear weapons and the dangerous balance of international politics suggest that the emphasis of Armistice-tide should be laid on repentance, reconciliation, and a determined self-dedication to a nobler future, rather than on past military victories with their appalling cost in young human lives.'[7]

[1] *Ibid.,* p.299.

[2] C. J. Cadoux, *The Early Church and the World: A History of the Christian Attitude to Pagan Society and the State Down to the Time of Constantinus* (T. & T. Clark, 1925).

[3] The white poppy was introduced by the Women's Co-operative Guild in 1933. Interest in the white poppy was revived in 1983, and again in 1986 for the International Year of Peace.

The red poppy was inspired by John McCrae's poem 'In Flanders field the poppies blow.' The poem was written in 1915, and the red poppy was adopted in 1921 by Field-Marshall Earl Haig. The first Poppy Day was 11 November 1921.

[4] Peace Pledge Union, 'Remembrance Weekend—Ideas for Action', an article in, *Remember and Disarm Action Information Pack* (1986)—available from Peace Pledge Union, 6 Endsleigh Street, London WC1.

[5] *Ibid.*

[6] *Ibid.,* article entitled 'Swimming Against the Tide'.

[7] *Ibid.*

What appears to be lacking in the writings of the Peace Pledge Union and in the symbolism of the white poppy is an adequate understanding of humanity. *The Times* editorial argued at a non-theological level:

'The white poppy brigade consists very largely of people who believe that to rid the world of war it is only necessary to renounce it. By laying white poppies rather than red on the Cenotaph they seek to express pity for those who died in the two World Wars, rather than pride in the successful defence of freedom and justice which so much tragic loss made possible. Above all, they seek to convey the message that those wars were due to the mere existence of armaments and warlike preparations, rather than to relative weakness and lack of unity among free nations.'[1]

Theologically we would argue that the doctrine of man gives us little cause to hope for a nobler future. At least the red poppy roots the symbolism firmly in the realities of history.[2]

Non-Pacifism

What of non-pacifism? Gill's clear distinction between state-related and personal-related responses is important. The pastor on Remembrance Sunday will be seeking to lead many whose decisions to fight rested on a subsuming of their personal feelings to duty to the state. To be morally defensible, it is argued that some notion of the Just War is fundamental. John Stott reduces the Just War requirements to three: the cause, which must be righteous; the means, which must be controlled; and the outcome, which must be reasonably predictable.[3]

The Just War concept, although pre-Christian was given a specifically Christian interpretation by Augustine in the fourth century. According to Stott this is the predominant position of Roman Catholicism and Protestantism today.[4] If so, it merits consideration as a backcloth to Remembrance Sunday. Implicit in the Just War concept is not only, as Bainton says, that 'Evil can be restrained by the coercive power of the state'[5], but that evil ought so to be restrained.

Gill, in assessing Augustine's texts, states 'The central thrust of Augustine's ethical argument is clearly deontological—war is morally justifiable because, in . . . of the Old Testament, God can be seen to command it.'[6]

Reinhold Niebuhr is one of the most powerful advocates of the Christian non-pacifist approach. At the outbreak of the Second World War, he went as far as to say 'that most modern forms of pacifism are heretical.'[7]

For Niebuhr, the non-pacifist approach 'is derived from an understanding to the Christian Gospel which refuses simply to equate the Gospel with the "law of love".'[8] He continues:

'Christianity is a religion which measures the total dimension of human existence not only in terms of the final norm of human conduct, which is expressed in the law of love, but also in terms of the fact of sin.'[9]

Niebuhr argues that it is because people are sinners 'justice can be achieved only by a certain degree of coercion on the one hand, and by resistance to coercion and tyranny on the other hand.'[10]

[1] *The Times* (8 November 1981), p.21.
[2] *The Times* (8 November 1986) p.21.
[3] John Stott, *Issues Facing Christians Today* (Marshalls, 1984) p.84.
[4] Stott, *Issues,* p.84.
[5] Roland H. Bainton, *Christian Attitudes Towards War and Peace* (Abingdon, New York, 1960) p.15.
[6] Gill, *A Textbook,* p.305.
[7] R. Niebuhr, *Why The Christian Church is Not Pacifist* (SCM, London, 1940) p.15.
[8] *Ibid.,* p.7.
[9] *Ibid.,* p.8.
[10] Niebuhr, p.23.

Many Christian non-pacifists would echo Niebuhr's conviction that discipleship requires not only turning the other cheek, but also the intention of 'securing justice in a sinful world.'[1] Indeed, we may note that Isaiah's 'day acceptable to the Lord' (Is. 58.5) requires loosing the chains of injustice and setting the oppressed free.

The danger of pacifism, for Niebuhr, is that it is a creed which appears to encourage faith in people rather than in God. He offers this illustration:
'If we believe that if Britain had only been fortunate enough to have produced 30 per cent instead of 2 per cent of conscientious objectors to military service, Hitler's heart would have been softened and he would not have dared to attack Poland, we hold a faith which no historic reality justifies.'

More recently Richard Harris has contributed effectively to the Christian non-pacifist stance. He insists 'Love is not incompatible with the use of restraining force.'[2] But, while some Christians will remain pacifist, 'resistance with weapons to the threat is for others an over-riding duty.'[3]

There is evident logical tension between the pacifist and non-pacifist stances. Specifically the difficulty would appear to reside in equating judgments on the acts of war with judgments on the purposes of war. A. R. Vidler sharpens the issue ethically. Pacifism, he points out, considers questions about the intrinsic quality of a certain kind of action. Non-pacifism, by contrast, seeks to answer questions about the best means of achieving desired results.[4] In other words, the pacifist and the non-pacifist positions highlight what can be described as a moral dualism between acts and ends—deontological and teleological ethics.

To give an example, Bainton is clearly arguing from a teleological position when he says:
'The most telling criticism against the pacifist is that by his refusal to destroy the oppressor he abandons the oppressed, because there are circumstances in which military intervention may terminate tyranny.'[5]
Oliver O'Donovan is arguing similarly when he asks 'What are we to do about international justice if we renounce the ultimate possibility of force?'[6] This would be the position of many who not only wear their medals with pride but also mourn lost relatives and friends.

Within the non-pacifist attitude to war, and in particular amongst those who fought and still suffer, can be discerned a strong feeling of necessity, of duty. That is, an approach which accepts non-pacifism with deep regret and reluctance; an attitude far removed from any concept of glorification of war. Many would admit that though they believed the wars had begun as 'Just Wars' gross injustices and deeds of obscene inhumanity were perpetuated by both sides.

A Canadian minister writing during the Second World War summed up:
'We expect nothing from the war except that everything sweet and precious will be crushed out of life for most of us. Nevertheless, we could do no other.'[7]

[1] *Ibid., p.16.*

[2] Richard Harris, *Christianity and War in a Nuclear Age* (Mowbray, 1986) p.9.

[3] *Ibid.,* p.50.

[4] A. R. Vidler, 'Theology of Pacifism' in Ashley Sampson, *This War And Christian Ethics: A Symposium* (Blackwell, Oxford, 1940) p.16ff.

[5] Bainton, p 250.

[6] Oliver O'Donovan, *In Pursuit of a Christian View of War* (Grove, Bramcote, 1977) p.19.

[7] Quoted in Bainton, p.221.

2. ATTITUDES TO REMEMBRANCE DAY

A pastor's attempt at innovation is often rebuffed with the cry 'but we've always done it this way!' Remembrance Day is one instance when this is not so.

The decision taken in 1946 to alter the actual day of remembrance to Sunday rather than the eleventh day of the eleventh month brought with it changes in attitude. Two minutes silence at 11 a.m. on a busy weekday, when the nation came almost to a literal standstill, was a powerful nationwide reminder of all that was achieved and lost in war, the debt owed, and the challenge to continue to work for justice and peace. By contrast, as *The Times* records 'Remembrance Sunday puts no-one to any inconvenience, but consequently it does not act as an effective reminder. It is just another Sunday.'[1]

It is pertinent to observe that on the continent, where countries suffered the additional rigours of invasion, occupation and consequent loss of freedom, remembrance is not an annual occurrence but a daily event:
'Willingness to remember, formally, the human cost of freedom is not confined to one day in a year. Every evening, at the tomb of the Unknown Warrior in Paris, under the Arc de Triomphe, the flame is ceremonially extinguished and rekindled. And at Ypres, every evening at 8 p.m. the traffic on the main road that passes through the Menin Gate is brought to a halt.'[1]

Detailed evidence of attitudes to Remembrance Day is difficult to glean. Perusal of articles in the *Baptist Times* and the *Church Times* provides some indication that attitudes have not always been as they are today.

The Baptist Times and attitudes to Remembrance Day

Analysis of the *Baptist Times* from 1919 to date provides the following evidence of changing attitudes to both war and to Remembrance Day itself.

In the twenty years between 1919 and 1938 in the weeks surrounding Armistice Day or Remembrance Day comment was made in the paper every year except for three years. In marked contrast, the subsequent twenty years between 1946 and 1965 saw a mere five years in which comment was made. The last twenty years have seen a resurgence of interest, with only five years lacking comment.

Trends can be discerned in the paper's approach to Remembrance Day. Pragmatism is evident in the years up to the 1930's. Remembrance was seen not only in terms of gratitude for the 'Great deliverance', but also as an annual spur to work hard for international peace and even harder to address the national economic and social issues—the aftermath of war.[3]

[1] *The Times* (8 November 1986) p.21.
[2] *Ibid.*
[3] For instance; *Baptist Times* (16 November 1923) p.795.

By 1935 a very different mood prevailed in the paper. One thought dominated, 'they did not die in vain.'[1] The very persistence of that strain evinces the doubts implied about the value of war.

Perhaps the most perturbing trend came in the late 1970's when nostalgia appears to have been the theme. Articles were based on recollections and requests were made for 'I remember' contributions from the readership.[2] Greater seriousness returned to the paper in the 1980's.[3]

The Church Times and attitudes to Remembrance Day

In the first few years after the First World War comment in the *Church Times* parallels that in the *Baptist Times*. Confidence that victory was God given, however, is more explicit in the *Church Times*. The edition after Armistice Day stated:

'The note of humble thanksgiving to Almighty God, which was heard all last week in the solemn services at crowded churches, on public platforms, in the street, in the houses, rose to a great crescendo in the Eucharists of Sunday. It was a signal proof that, deep down in the people's heart lies a profound belief in a Divine overruling power.'[4]

The same edition also prints the sermon preached on Sunday 17 November, the preacher taking the text 'The Lord hath been mindful of us, and He will bless us.' (Psalm 115.12) It concluded 'Thanks be to God, who giveth us the victory through Jesus Christ.'[5]

In these early years the *Church Times* offered its readership guidance on how to approach Armistice Day, as advised by the Archbishops of Canterbury and York. For instance, the two minutes silence was to be observed as:

'An act of solemn remembrance and recollection—remembrance of the men who, in a time of war, were faithful unto death: recollection of the duty laid upon us for whom they died to see that these men shall not have died in vain.'[6]

The Archbishops of Canterbury and York suggested further that the following Sunday be a day of special prayer:

Let prayers rise in every church through the land for a fuller and wider coming of that spirit of justice and brotherhood among all nations and classes whereby alone the peace, heralded by the signing of the Armistice two years ago, can be made secure.'[7]

Also, in common with the *Baptist Times,* concern was expressed for peace within the industrial life of Great Britain.

After the Second World War, death, or the theology of death was a focus accompanied by the refrain 'By the great mercy of God, you and I are spared.'[8]

[1] For instance; *Baptist Times* (11 November 1937) first page.
[2] For instance; *Baptist Times* (11 November 1976) p.6.
[3] For instance; *Baptist Times* (5 November 1981) p.2.
[4] *Church Times* (22 November 1918), p.375.
[5] *Church Times* (22 November 1918), p.380.
[6] *Church Times* (5 November 1920) p.438.
[7] *Ibid.*
[8] *Church Times* (9 November 1945) p.642.

In 1976, a year when *Baptist Times* readers were encouraged 'to remember', the *Church Times* included a devotional article of considerable depth and insight. Remembrance Sunday was not to be effaced from the calendar, but faced square on:

> 'This is why we keep Remembrance Sunday in the presence of God. There are some things with which only God can deal, and one is man's warring nature. So Remembrance Sunday turns itself into a day of penitence, a plea for forgiveness and a readiness to accept the Grace of God, to amend our lives according to his holy Word.'[1]

The depth of that article is to be contrasted with some more recent thoughts. Particularly difficult is the restatement of the parallel sometimes suggested between the death of Christ and those who died in war. Thus, we read in 1981 'We commemorate the self-giving of so many millions who died for their fellow-men' juxtaposed with 'At every celebration of the Holy Communion we remember his supreme sacrifice.'[2]

Attitudes to war and Remembrance Day have certainly changed. In 1958 the *Baptist Times* pointedly observed that though we might no longer glorify war 'We should not become blind to the fact that our changed attitude, as well as our precious liberties, owe much to those who laid down their lives, who fought bravely to the end, and who so suffered.'[3] Put another way, it could be argued that the freedom to be a pacifist in Britain in the 1980's, is in part attributable to those who fought for such 'precious liberties.'

Whatever our theoretical attitude to war in general, we must, in considering Remembrance Sunday, address ourselves to the reality that our present national and international order is causally related to the outcome of the two world wars. Michael Walker addressed this issue in this prayer:

> 'Lord, as we turn in horror from war may we not turn away from those who, before our birth fought our battles. We can renounce war, because we are free; we are free, because our fathers fought and died.'[1]

According to Keith Clements, this notion of freedom is especially close to the British heart. As such Remembrance Sunday is a part of what he describes as the 'cultural story of Britain':

> 'the one word which most British people would, if asked, say is what the country stands for . . . [is] . . . freedom. There will not be universal agreement as to the extent to which freedom is enjoyed in Britain today, or even as to what freedom consists of. But it is the argument about freedom which is the link in so much of the political, religious, social and cultural story of Britain.'

We noted towards the beginning of this section the practice of Remembrance on the continent. We must also conclude looking beyond the British Isles, reminding ourselves to avoid generalizations about the present world order. There are still too many wars, too many prisoners of conscience and too many nations where inhumanity reigns. Many people are rightly critical of Remembrance Sunday today in so far as thanksgiving for our freedom myopically misses the plight of so many others.

[1] *Church Times* (12 November 1976) p.11.
[2] *Church Times* (6 November 1981), p.8.
[3] *Baptist Times* (6 November 1958), p.5.
[4] *Baptist Times* (6 November, 1969).
[5] Keith W. Clements, *A Patriotism For Today: Dialogue With Dietrich Bonhoeffer*, (Baptist College, Bristol, 1984) p.81.

3. REMEMBRANCE AS A DUTY

Since many Christians have accepted some notion of the Just War, can we allow a Remembrance service that so subordinates any idea of victory for that just cause, that the very presupposition is implicitly rejected? There must be some positive remembrance of the past. We may prefer to forget war and focus on peace, but as Stott has said 'The quest for peace with justice is much more costly than appeasement.'[1]

That cost can be understood in terms of duty, both in respect to the duty of those who fought and our duty to remember. The point may be sharpened by reversing the question and asking if there could have been a duty not to fight. Faced, for example, with the Nazi determination to annihilate the Jews, could we legitimately and morally have allowed them to be utterly destroyed?

The basis of duty is understood in this booklet as residing in the divine nature and will of God, rather than as being self-imposed or imposed by society. Acknowledging God as Creator necessitates the rooting of our thoughts and actions in the reality of the physical as well as spiritual world. Acknowledging God as Sustainer necessitates recognition of God's sovereignty over the past, the present and the future. Acknowledging that God is not only Love but Justice precludes an attitude to peace that ignores justice.

This duty to remember would appear to be a biblical notion. Indeed, the biblical record has been described as evincing a 'ministry of memory.'[2] Days of remembering the Lord and all he had done for Israel were to be marked by penitence, thanksgiving and resolve.

Even as God commanded Israel to remember and to keep on remembering, so arguably we are commanded to remember. Not, we hasten to add, to suggest a direct parallel between that special convenantal relationship that God had with Israel and his relationship with Britain. In the former case, the Israelites are encouraged to remember the mighty acts of God, not some victory they themselves had achieved. For the Christian worshipper the true remembrance is not to remember the glory of the dead, rather the glory of God. Nevertheless, the Israelites did also remember their fathers.

Be that as it may, we cannot dismiss out of hand the parallel between the Israelites' call to remember the way in which God delivered them from the oppression and tyranny of Egypt, and the way in which so much of mankind was delivered from oppression and tyranny through two world wars. If part of one's duty as a Christian is seen in terms of working for the removal of injustice and tyranny, then, with all its problems, remembrance of those who contributed to that end is equally our duty.

The traditional singing of Isaac Watts' hymn 'Our God, our help in ages past' reflects an acceptance of the need to remember at a 'folk' religious level. But the need to remember is also valid on a secular level in so far as we are constituted by our memories. The maxim 'lest we forget' is as much for everyday living as for Remembrance.

[1] Stott, *Issues,* p.83.
[2] *Baptist Times* (5 November 1953) p.2.

If there is a duty to remember, then we need to clarify what it is we are remembering on Remembrance Sunday. In Britain today it is difficult for most people to appreciate the importance of victory in 1918 and 1945, for society throughout much of the world at those times. *The Times* in 1920 spelt out the 'enemy' defeated. Significantly, the enemy was not perceived as a people but as a philosophy—militarism . . .

'the blasphemous and inhuman doctrine that might is right, and that the state, as the incarnation of might, stands above the moral law. The overthrow of the doctrine was indispensable to the survival of public morality among men. It was fatal to liberty and to all those virtues which flourish among the free . . . no greater issue has been committed to the fortunes of arms; none has been fought at such terrible cost . . . They were confident that the cause of right would win; win or lose, they were resolved to do their duty . . . We celebrate the victory with immeasurable thankfulness; wonder and awe . . . not hatred or passion, greed or ambition, moved our peoples. It was duty and duty only . . . the war had to be, because plain duty forbade us, above all others, to renounce justice and all right by cowardly acquiescence in a monstrous crime.'[1]

After the Second World War we were encouraged 'To recall the sacrifice of those who made it possible for us to survive.'[2] So long as it can be argued that our present freedom is attributable to those who achieved it, have we not a moral duty to acknowledge that?

Oliver O'Donovan, in a published sermon, suggests that what we ought to be remembering on Remembrance Sunday cannot be simply those who died, for we all die; nor can it be only the horrors of war, for there are other horrors caused by mankind, such as road deaths. Rather, O'Donovan would have us focus on the meaning of war, and what they did who lost their lives in it. He places war in the context of Psalm 46 and 'the works of the Lord.'

In the Old Testament, O'Donovan argues, God's peace is inconceivable without God's judgment; 'peace is never amoral; it is founded on judgment and righteousness.' Even though victory is claimed by one side, justice is vindicated only in the recognition that both sides perpetuated wrong: 'To think of war in terms of justice, then, exposes us not only to gladness but to self-criticism.' Hence, he argues, 'To remember war as the arbitration of right and wrong is to accept the task of specific thankfulness and specific self-criticism' and it is the role of the church 'to foster this thankfulness and this penitence.'[3]

Norman Pittenger, writing at the outbreak of World War Two, draws attention to the breadth of such notions as justice, and indeed truth, and consequently the breadth of the notion of duty:

'There may be some truth in the enemy's cause, some justice: let us be ready to pray for the enemy, and in that way recognize the truth

---

[1] *The Times* (11 November 1920), p.11.
[2] *The Expository Times,* 59 (1947-1948) p.21
[3] Oliver O'Donovan, 'Remembrance Sunday', in *Third Way* vol. 6 no. 10 (1983), pp.6-7.

and the justice. Only in that way can we hope for a peace which in the end may endure, because it is founded upon the claims of truth and justice and not upon pettiness and hate, revenge and retaliation.'[1]

Acknowledging that justice and truth, injustice and lies were not the sole preserve of one side, greatly helps determine the atmosphere of a Remembrance service, by precluding simplisitic notions of glorification and patriotism. Robert Clark is surely stating a truth when he says 'A Christian can thank God for accomplishing his will through the evil doings of man.'[2] We must eschew, however, all suggestions that such evil resided or still resides in specific nations or peoples. It is not only pastorally unhelpful to continue to talk of the Germans, the Japanese—or even the Argentinians—as 'the enemy', when they may well be in our congregations—but such an attitude is morally suspect as racist.

Will there be a continuing duty to observe Remembrance Sunday? Each year the situation changes. Fewer people can recall directly the two world wars. We argue that the notion of duty does not permit a ready rejection of Remembrance. Admittedly the focus on the two world wars will ultimately become relatively meaningless. Still, however, there are widows and others who suffer because of the First World War. For many years to come there will be people profoundly affected by the Second World War.

Across the world many peoples are presently enduring the horrors of war. Remembrance Sunday is one day in the Church calendar which can be set aside specifically for remembering all such peoples. The responsibility of pastors to encourage their congregations to be peacemakers must root such encouragement in the realities of the past. That requires the recognition that, in the past, Christians have seen peacemaking as possible only through the military defeat of evil and injustice.

---

[1] Norman W. Pittenger, 'Prayer in Wartime' in Sampson, *This War,* p.40.
[2] Robert E. D. Clark, 'The Case For All-Out Pacifism', in Oliver R. Barclay, *Pacifism and War* (IVP, Leicester, 1984) p.100.

13

4. THE PASTOR

Know Thyself! The bemedalled pastor, the pacifist pastor, and the young pastor all have obvious potential difficulties on Remembrance Sunday: in the first case, the danger of glorifying war, in the second, that of denying the realities of human fallibility, and in the third case, lack of experience.

The more military-minded pastor needs to be sensitive to the pastoral needs of the pacifists in the congregation, and not least to the pastoral needs of those whose suffering stems from conscientious objection.

By contrast could a pacifist pastor lead a Remembrance service without compromising personal integrity? Should not such a pastor rather, offer an alternative 'Peace Service', or even lead his or her congregation on a peace march? But before pacifist pastors decide not to share in Remembrance Sunday services, they ought to consider afresh their pastoral responsibility to their flock. The pastoral calling is the prior calling to which personal attitudes to pacifism and non-pacifism must be subordinated.

The young pastor can be encouraged by this emphasis on pastoral responsibility. Conversations about 'the war' with older members of the congregation in their own homes will soon reveal the depths of experience evoked by the Remembrance Sunday service. That at least is the situation likely to obtain for the next ten years or so.

What the pastor wears on Remembrance Sunday is important. Decisions need to be taken—Should medals be worn if you have them? Do you put on a poppy, and if so, is it to be a red one, a white one, or both? Whether we are prepared to admit it, or not, these things become part of the message the congregation receives, and as such can either hinder or help worship. Drawing attention to these things by, for instance, explaining to the children and young people our decision, has the double advantage of involving them while also answering some of the unspoken questions in the minds of older peple.

Assured leadership is also particularly important in this service. The congregation needs to feel not only accepted but secure, confident that things will not go wrong with, for example, the timing of the two minutes silence.

It should be noted that these remarks apply not simply to the pastor, but to all who may share the leadership of the Remembrance Sunday service.

5. THE CONGREGATION

What we prepare for Remembrance Sunday should be influenced, in part, by our expectations of who will be present, the congregation. We need to take into account both the traditions of the church and its geographical location. As a generalization, it would seem that traditions are strongest in rural areas, weakest in the inner city, and most ambivalent in the suburbs.

Remembrance Sunday is one of those special occasions when pastors can expect to find present people who attend church infrequently, and perhaps only on this one Sunday in the year. They can also expect to discover regular members wearing different hats—literally as well as figuratively. The international background of some members of the congregation becomes of greater significance than on other Sundays.

Some people will be coming with polished medals, some in uniform, active members of the armed forces, some representing voluntary defence organizations, members of the Territorial Army, members of British Legion, others attired in civic regalia, and yet others may be present because they feel it is part of their cultural heritage.

In apparent opposition to all these folks the pastor can expect the Peace People. And in the congregation there will be also the young people and children.

We need to ask many questions about this complex gathering of peoples. What are they saying—to themselves, to each other, to the pastor and to God? What are they feeling—grief, anger guilt, anxiety, pride, patriotism? What are they remembering—past anger, guilt, loss? What are their needs? Perhaps, for all present, the greatest need is to feel accepted—by each other, by the pastor, by God, and therefore able to accept themselves because God's acceptance is proclaimed.

The weeks before and after Remembrance Sunday can be crucial in ministering to the needs of the congregation. Preparation for the regular members of the congregation could include taking some aspect of remembrance on the previous Sunday, teaching and discussions in house groups, youth groups and in Sunday School.

In the week following Remembrance Sunday, space ought to be given for pastoral visits by the pastor and any other members of the pastoral team, to those in need of special care at this time.

Relating the Remembrance service to young people is a particular problem. The regular young people would greatly benefit from being prepared for the day either in their classes on the previous Sunday, or in their mid-week meeting. Teenagers can be expected to find most Remembrance services bewildering, and yet the service raises issues which are close to their hearts—right and wrong, justice and injustice, life and death, peace, and how to live and think as a young Christian in a world of strife.

Fortunately, there are plenty of resources available to develop young people's awareness. Discussions could be stimulated by studying together an order of service. A suitable and willing older member of the congregation, with first hand experience of war and suffering, could be invited to share with the young people the meaning of remembrance. Reading and responding to the war poems of Rupert Brooke, Wilfred Owen and Siegfried Sassoon, is sure to stimulate. Wilfred Owens 'Dulce et Decorum' is included in an anthology designed for children aged from nine to fifteen.[1]

For a more active approach to the young people, they could prepare and perform the dramatic prayer 'The Litany of War.'[2] Even more active learning could be derived from some of the ideas and games in Bob Moffett's books *Crowdbreakers* and its sequel *Crowdmakers*.[3]

The leader of the young people needs to be particularly well prepared and sensitive. The issue of death in war, for instance, may be painful if one of the group is grieving over a personal bereavement. The idealist zeal of the young can be practically channelled into applying reconciliation amongst their peer group in the area (especially appropriate where the area comprises marked racial and social differences), and of course, at home. More broadly, this enthusiasm can be directed to greater awareness of the world beyond the British Isles. Patrick Johnstone's prayer guide, *Operation World,* is to be highly recommended.[4]

[1] M. Harrison and C. Stuart-Clark, *The New Dragon Book of Verse* (OUP, 1977).
[2] P. Burbridge and M. Watts, *Red Letter Days,* (Hodder & Stoughton, 1986) pp.172-177.
[3] Bob Moffett, *Crowdbreakers,* (Pickering 1983), *Crowdmakers,* (Pickering 1985).
[4] Patrick Johnstone, *Operation World* (STC/WEC 1986, fourth edition).

6. THE REMEMBRANCE SERVICE

Our Remembrance service ought to be, first and foremost, a service of worship. Colin Buchanan's booklet, *Leading Worship,* is particularly apposite.[1] The pastor is ultimately responsible for determining the aim, structure and content of the worship. Due time and attention must be given to preparation with all who may be involved, in leadership on the day, such as the musicians and readers, as well as those responsible for preparing the church, such as flower arrangers and banner groups.

No single published order of service for Remembrance Sunday has been discovered which can be recommended unequivocally. Given the evident problems with the service, that fact is not surprising.

As a starting point, we can adopt the guidelines offered by the Archbishops of Canterbury and York in 1949. They suggested three foci for Remembrance Sunday, which could be described as three expressions of our duty under the sovereignty of God:
> 'Thanksgiving for a great deliverance, faithful remembrance of all who suffered and made their sacrifice to gain it, dedication of ourselves to the grave responsibility which rests upon us to work for and win good order, right dealing, harmony and peace in all human relationships inside our own nation and throughout the world.'[2]

They conclude with what could be called their fourth focus, 'The word for us all is "be still and know that I am God." '

We shall examine three published orders of service, one Baptist, one commended for use by the Archbishops of Canterbury and York, and one not so approved.

Strictly, the Baptist contribution is a selection of sentences and prayers, rather than a complete order of service; its value resides in the content of the selections rather than their order. The order, as given is: Sentences; Invocation; Confession; The Scripture Lessons; Thanksgiving; Supplication; For the Forces; For the Victims of War; Commemoration.

Persual of Payne and Winward's *Orders and Prayers for Church Worship,* highlights a marked discrepancy between the popular recollections of Remembrance services as glorifications of war, and their own careful suggestions.[3] There may be a denominational factor, though it must be stressed that conclusions cannot be made at present. Pittenger, for instance, in 1939, quoting from the Collects in the Book of Common Prayer, confessed that he felt the church 'has sinned grievously' in this matter.[4] William Temple, in 1944, by contrast, refused to pray for victory unless the phrase 'if it be Thy will' were added, as indeed could be found in the 1928 Prayer Book.[5]

---

[1] Colin Buchanan, *Leading Worship,* (Grove Worship Series no. 76, Grove Books, 1981 and 1987).

[2] *The Times,* (6 October 1949).

[3] E. A. Payne and S. F. Winward, *Orders and Prayers for Church Worship* (Carey Kingsgate Press, London, 1960), pp.116-119.

[4] Pittenger, *Prayer in Wartime,* p.30.

[5] F. S. Temple (ed.), *William Temple: Some Lambeth Letters* (OUP, 1963), p.145.

There is much to commend in Payne and Winward's work. The *Invocation* focuses on the sovereignty of God, 'Lord of life and vanquisher of death', and encourages us to thank God for all that has been done for us. The prayer of *Confession* focuses on our sins against God, and, like the Lord's Prayer, asks for forgiveness 'as we forgive them that trespass against us'. It is difficult to glorify war in such a setting of true confession and forgiveness. In *Thanksgiving* again the focus is on what God has done. In line with the Archbishops' outline, the prayer closes with the request that we might be 'good citizens of our country and loyal servants of Thine eternal kingdom.'

In 1968 was published 'A Service For Remembrance Sunday', which was 'Commended for general use by the Archbishops of Canterbury and York, and of Wales, the Cardinal Archbishop of Westminster, and the Moderator of the Free Church Federal Council.'[1] This comprises a full order of service with an alternative form of the Act of Remembrance. The order, as given is: Introduction; Hymn; Lesson; Hymn; Act of Penitence; Intercession; Hymn; Sermon; Hymn; Act of Remembrance; Act of Commitment; The Lord's Prayer; National Anthem; Blessing; Act of Remembrance (Alternative Form); Hymns.

This is an excellent resource, offering a wide choice of hymns and lessons in addition to the prayers. It even offers some guidance on timing and when the collection may be taken. Particularly attractive are the following features. First, the *Introduction* which leaves the congregation in no doubt as to the purpose of this service. It begins 'We are here to worship Almighty God, whose purposes are good, whose power sustains the world he has made'. Second, the clear and appropriate prayers of confession and intercession. Thirdly, the frequent instructions for times of silence, other than the two minutes silence.

In 1982, Church Society also published an order of service entitled 'A Service for Remembrance Sunday'.[2] The publishers acknowledge 'It has not been approved for general use in the Church of England by either the General Synod or the Archbishops of Canterbury and York.' Their order is: Introduction; Hymn; Confession; Psalm; Act of Remembrance; Reading from the Old Testament; The Jubilate; Reading from the New Testament; Hymn; The Creed; Prayers; Hymn; The Address; Hymn; The Blessing; The National Anthem.

Like its namesake, this order can be used as a quarry. Again, the timing is spelt out. The *Introduction* begins with triumphant words of Psalm 9 'The Lord reigns forever . . .'. Most helpfully, the prayers of confession are introduced with some of Jesus's words 'love your enemies and pray for those who persecute you.' The congregation is also given guidance on what to think during the silence itself.

[1] *A Service for Remembrance Sunday* (SPCK, 1968 and 1984).
[2] *A Service for Remembrance Sunday* (Church Society, 1982).

7. THE ACT OF REMEMBRANCE

For many, this is the heart of a Remembrance Service. Sometimes it is treated as an isolated unit in an otherwise unrelated service. Some churches alter the time of their morning service to ensure that the two minutes silence begins at 11 a.m. Although the 11 a.m. timing is not essential, it is powerfully symbolic, not only in complying with the original hour of the Armistice, but more so as many thousands stand together in silence at the one time. Whenever the service begins, ample time needs to be given to prepare the congregation for the Act itself, to ensure that it is a natural part of the order of worship for that day.

At the heart of this section is undoubtedly the two minutes' silence. In the SPCK order this silence is surrounded by nothing more than an introductory sentence and a subsequent prayer. In their Alternative order, this basic pattern is expanded as follows: After the introduction it is recommended that a list of those to be remembered is read. This is followed by Laurence Binyon's words

'They shall grow not old, as we that are left grow old:
Age shall not weary them, nor the years condemn.
At the going down of the sun and in the morning
we will remember them.'

The congregation is encouraged to repeat the last words, 'We will remember them'. Then comes the silence, followed by the closing prayer. They suggest that the Last Post and the Reveille may be sounded after the silence.

The Church Society order begins the Act of Remembrance with verses from Psalm 103, before following a similar pattern to the SPCK Alternative order, with the exception that the Last Post precedes the silence, and there is no closing prayer.

What ought we to encourage the congregation to do in the two minutes silence? Payne and Winward's introductory words are direct, and with the exception of the word 'brethren', uncontroversial. 'Brethren, let us remember in silence before God, all those who died in the two World Wars.'

The SPCK order contains a theological difficulty in the encouragement given to the congregation to 'commend to his sure keeping those who have died . . .' That could be interpreted as Universalism.

More helpfully, the Church Society order suggests that the two minutes silence be spent praying for the war bereaved, those suffering because of past wars, for present areas of trouble, and for peace.

In 1938 readers of the *Baptist Times* were encouraged to spend the two minutes trying to answer the question 'what can I do to promote peace?'[1] A desire to focus in worship away from war and towards peace is laudible. But, to attempt to be peacemakers without facing up to the realities of history is to build castles in the air.

Children present for the two minutes silence can be encouraged to share in the experience by spending the time, for example, thinking about the sadness of war, of boys and girls who have been made orphans, of children they have seen on television, and by thanking God for the peace that we have.

---

[1] *Baptist Times* (10 November 1938).

8. PRAYERS

'Lord teach us to pray' is a request of special urgency on Remembrance Sunday. Pitfalls are numerous, and the pastor or persons leading prayer need to be especially aware of their own feelings towards the service. A careless word or phrase can greatly mar the worship. For this reason we commend the use of written prayers.

The fact that many published remembrance prayers can be criticized is a salutary reminder of the difficulty of such prayer and the risks of extemporary prayer. This is not to deny the Spirit, rather it is to affirm his guiding hand as we spend time preparing for the service. On Sunday the pastor's task is to lead the congregation in prayer, not to offer private prayers in public.

Examination of the language of our prayers is a vital part of preparation. The vocabulary of sacrifice is particularly problematic. The number of people who willingly laid down their lives as a sacrifice must have been very few indeed. In simple terms, most fought to survive, not to die. Many fought, as we have noted, out of some sense of duty, and they too intended to survive. It is better, therefore, to pray about those who were killed or who died, rather than about those who laid down their lives or sacrificed themselves.

A second, related problem area is the tendency to refer only to those who died in active service. Civilians were also killed, and this was true even in the Falklands.

A third aspect of language which can irritate is the use of words and phrases which are deemed sexist. Whether they are or not is beside the point—the pastoral heart must acknowledge how people react, not how they ought to react. But, it is important to do this unobtrusively. Thus we can pray 'that all may . . .' or 'that all people may . . .' rather than 'that all men may . . .'.

Prayers of repentance and confession are obviously vital, yet they pose problems which need to be recognized. Even though we believe in forgiveness and reconciliation, there does seem to be a need to repeat annually our confessions of sin and guilt. But in such prayers we must be careful not to doubt the validity of the wars remembered. Such an attitude suggests that those who fought, by fighting are sinning, and presumably in dying remained unforgiven. Even Temple, whilst desiring that the opening mood of a potential victory service ought to be one of penitence, nevertheless also said:

> 'If we believe that in fact the overthrow of what Hitler stands for is for the welfare of mankind, even though one might prefer that it should be accomplished through other means, I find it hard to see how one could refrain from giving thanks for the victories.[1]

As O'Donovan puts it 'I find nothing particularly Christian in a liturgical celebration of ambivalence'.[1]

In our concern for language, we must not overlook the importance of silence in prayer, other than in the two minutes itself. Especially in a service of remembrance there is need to give the congregation space to think and pray, and the Holy Spirit freedom to prompt them beyond the spoken prayers. A short time of silence is to be commended within and after spoken prayers of thanksgiving, confession and intercession.

[1] Temple, *William Temple*, p.71.
[2] O'Donovan, 'Remembrance Sunday', p.7.

There are several very good books available which can be used as resources for Remembrance Sunday prayers, in addition to those recorded in the published orders of service. Especially valuable are Frank Colquhoun's books; *Parish Prayers, Contemporary Parish Prayers* and *New Parish Prayers.*[1] All three are to be commended as works including prayers appropriate for public use. Most pastors would wish to modernize the English in Parish Prayers, and many would find it necessary to alter the odd word or phrase. The overall range in the three books, however, is sufficiently broad to offer invaluable assistance for the pastor or leader of prayers. Dick Williams' *Prayers for Today's Church*[2] has only a few prayers specifically for remembrance, but for the pastor keen to use the overhead projector or photocopy responsive prayers, this work has the advantage of some degree of freedom from copyright.

Time spent studying all these books on prayer is time well spent. For instance, Colquhoun's *Contemporary Parish Prayers* has not only a section specifically for Remembrance Sunday but includes eminently suitable prayers and prayer ideas under the headings: The Nations of the World; Our Own Nation; People in Need; Funerals and Memorial Services.

How these prayers are led is as important as the words and silences used. One's imagination can be used with due care. For instance, intercessory prayers for specific trouble spots in the world could be introduced with a well-produced overhead map. Again, with even greater care and preparation, leadership of the prayers of confession could be shared between Christian representatives of former enemies.

---

[1] Frank Colquhoun, *Parish Prayers* (Hodder and Stoughton, 1967), *Contemporary Parish Prayers* (Hodder and Stoughton, 1975), *New Parish Prayers* (Hodder and Stoughton, 1982).

[2] Dick Williams, *Prayers for Today's Church,* (CPAS, 1972).

9. THE SERMON

In *Preaching On Special Occasions*, Charles Hutchins observes that the pastor, when the less committed are more likely to be present, has much more going against him'.[1] Perhaps this is more true within the Church of England than in Non-Conformist traditions. Hutchins subsumes Remembrance Sunday under the heading 'Civic Occasions'.

Faced with Mayoral entries into the church and rows of the uniformed within the congregation, Hutchins asks how the uniqueness of Christ is to be proclaimed. He suggests four objectives to aid the preacher: (1) To make the occasion meaningful. (2) to proclaim God's relevance. (3) To explain God's demands. (4) To elicit man's response.[2]

One approach to preaching on Remembrance Sunday is to tackle one of the major issues head on. For instance pacifism and non-pacifism. When handling potentially controversial topics in the pulpit, Stott encourages us to be 'authoritative in expounding biblical principles, but tentative in applying them to the complex issues of the day'.[3] With the complex and profound pastoral needs present wihin many congregations on Remembrance Sunday, there is little justification for treating the pulpit as a platform for pacifism or militarism.

That being the case, Stott asks how we can be 'brave not cowardly, humble not dogmatic, and prudent not foolish?'[4] His answer is to preach in such a way as 'to help Christians to develop a Christian mind'.[5] This is to be achieved in four stages. First, the preacher is to expound fearlessly the biblical principles. Secondly, to summarize alternative Christian applications. Thirdly, to indicate, if wise, the preacher's own stance. Fourthly, to leave the congregation free to make up its own mind.

On Remembrance Sunday the biblical principle of the Justice of God must be prominent. Such alternative responses as pacifism and the Just War argument can be described, leaving each person open to make his or her conclusion, though in no doubt about the duty of remembrance.

Another, arguably more pastoral, approach to preaching on Remembrance Sunday derives from the evident parallel with a funeral service. Ian Bunting's booklet, *Preaching at Funerals,* is of considerable value in this respect. We would do well to consider the three issues which he suggests ought to be before the preacher at a funeral service. Namely 'the certainty and seriousness of death, the hope of resurrection, and the ultimate unity of all believers in Christ'.[6] We may add, Christ the healer of memories.

If peace is to be the theme of the sermon, it ought not to be an abstract notion of peace, but the objective truth of the Prince of Peace. Similarly such themes as justice and truth must be rooted in the Godhead. For to do otherwise is to encourage faith in humanity not in God. We must make clear that the only valid answers derive from the eternal dimension.

[1] Charles H. Hutchins, *Preaching on Special Occasions* (Grove Worship Series No. 89, Grove Books, 1984), p.5.
[2] *Ibid.,* p.14.
[3] John R. W. Stott, *I Believe In Preaching* (Hodder and Stoughton, 1982) p.178.
[4] Stott, *I Believe,* p.170.
[5] *Ibid.*
[6] Ian Bunting, *Preaching at Funerals* (Grove Booklet on Ministry and Worship No. 62, Grove Books, 1978), pp.7-12.

10. THE EUCHARIST

What ought to be the primary focus of our Remembrance Service? Pittenger has offered a constructive way in which we can look to Christ and find in him a principle.

'As Christians, we should never forget that our very *locus standi* is as members of the Body of Christ, which includes all those who are redeemed, even our enemy, and that will prevent us from hating our brother (either actually in the faith, or potentially as one for whom Christ died) even when our situation in sin makes some terrible duty a necessity.'[1]

If Pittenger, in wartime, could speak of the Body of Christ as a focus of unity, how much more today could the Eucharist or Lord's Supper be seen as the true focus of Remembrance Sunday worship.

To focus the Remembrance Sunday service on the Eucharist undoubtedly raises theological and practical issues. The principal theological issue would appear to be whether the Eucharist is understood as the means or as the basis of Christian unity. We would argue that it can be both. For Christians in particular the Eucharist expresses that tension between unity in Christ that is now, and the unity in Christ that is yet to be.

For both Christians and uncommitted people in the congregation the Eucharist can also be a symbol pointing to the objective truth of peace revealed in the person of the Prince of Peace. The invitation to partake comes from Christ himself, the one who 'welcomes sinners, and eats with them' (Luke 15.2).

It is an act of worship which offers hope to all who respond to Christ's invitation. But equally it is an act that proclaims that true peace is ultimately by grace alone, grace which comes through the suffering, the love and the justice of the cross.

Practical problems implicit in focusing on the Eucharist include the constraints of some church constitutions on both the frequency and openness to non-members. Wherever the pastor or president is not constrained they can sensitively and clearly explain to the whole congregation that the invitation is truly the Lord's and they are individually free to respond by receiving the elements.

The pastor or president should also initiate 'the Peace', encouraging all to take part; this could be a very special moment for those who feel unable to take the elements to experience something of the meaning of unity in Christ, the Prince of Peace. Indeed, in churches where the Eucharist is not possible on Remembrance Sunday, 'the Peace' can come initiated anyway.

Churches could specifically invite and welcome members of nations once described as enemies. For at this table all Christians of whatever race, whatever history, are commanded to obey that great duty to share the bread and wine in memory of Christ, and in so doing, practice the oneness of the Body of Christ on earth.

In such a service, all can sincerely offer thanks for deliverance from that which was evil, unjust and tyrannical; all can offer thanks for those who died obedient to duty within the limits of their understanding; all can seek fresh forgiveness and reconciliation. All, in Christ, can find the one foundation, the one rock on which peacemakers can build. Our worship and endeavours can then be placed in the eschatological hope of the consummated kingdom when 'Nation will not take up sword against nation, nor will they train for war any more' (Isaiah 2.4).

[1] Pittenger, 'Prayer in Wartime', p.43.

11. CONCLUSION

'Christianity is seen as eirenic, but not quietistic: it involves an uneasy tension between "peace" and "justice"'.[1] Remembrance Sunday focuses this tension.

If we approach Remembrance Sunday ethically, in terms of our motive, the means, and the probable result, we may go some way towards easing this tension. The motive, we have suggested, is that of duty—duty to thank God for the victory of justice over injustice, and for those who fought and suffered in that cause; duty to seek forgiveness for the injustices of all; duty to seek reconciliation; duty to be peacemakers; duty especially in this context, to acknowledge God as Creator, Sustainer and Redeemer.

The means must be commensurate with true worship. This does not necessarily preclude militaria, for that is to judge; but it does demand great sensitivity. The Eucharist offers a primary focus.

The result: 'A day acceptable to the Lord'. In the context of Isaiah 58 that requires a profoundly realistic as well as spiritual interpretation of such a concept as setting the oppressed free. Peacemaking ought to be earthed in the Body of Christ—where there is neither Jew nor Gentile, British nor German . . .

Our duty, as pastors is not to gratify the demands of those who would glorify war, nor the thoroughgoing pacifist. Rather, our duty is to offer a day acceptable to the Lord, and only in this way may we, in conscience, respond to the pastoral issues consequent upon Remembrance.

The observance of Remembrance Sunday is not by definition the glorification of war; that it is often seen as such is not a valid reason for forgetting it. For the moral difficulties of not observing Remembrance Sunday in some form as suggested may be of much greater import. The Holocaust is an horrific reminder that there are occasions when peacemaking only has meaning in the paradox of war.

[1] Gill, *A Textbook*, p.413.

APPENDIX 1: RESOURCES

Much useful material can be found in the works already cited this booklet. In this section I will mention sermon outlines given in those works, and then list a selection of remembrance lessons and hymns. in selecting relatively short readings, I am awre of the need to consider carefully their context. In Psalm 137, for instnace, remembrance would appear to incite vengeance!

Charles Hutchins offers two Remembrance Sunday sermon outlines in *Preaching On Special Occasions*. Furthermore, at least two of the funeral sermon outlines in Ian Bunting's *Preaching At Funerals* could be readily adapted: specifically, Sermon 1, 'The Pain Of Love', based on 1 Corinthians 13.12; and Sermon 3, 'Creation Waits . . .', using Romans 8.19, 21.